Spare-Time Fortune Guide

Spare-Time Fortune Guide

Duane G. Newcomb

Parker Publishing Co., Inc.   West Nyack, New York

Library of Congress Cataloging in Publication Data

```
Newcomb, Duane G
    Spare-time fortune guide.

    Bibliography:  p.
    1.  Success.  2.  Business.  3.  Self-employed.
I.  Title.
HF5386.N38            650'.12            73-6805
ISBN 0-13-824185-6
```

What This Book Will Do For You

We are today on the verge of the greatest opportunity explosion this country has ever seen. And within the next few years, thousands of new fortunes will be made—*one of them could be yours.*

It's not necessary to have more time or money. You don't have to quit your present job, if you have one, nor do you need anything more beyond what you already possess to get started.

The question, of course, is how do I start? Exactly how do I take that first step? How do I manage myself so I can take off on the big money path and keep right on going?

That's what this book is all about. It's your step-by-step guide to making a big money fortune in *your spare time.* It starts you where you are: on your present job, working for somebody else, in a business that's going nowhere, or out of work and flat broke, and shows you how to re-orient yourself with big-money know-how, and build quickly from there to riches.

The first section shows you how to see big-money possibilities everywhere—how to lay out a skeleton money action system—how to appraise your own money-making skills—how to set yourself a money goal—and exactly how to put your success mechanism to work to springboard you to riches—*all in your spare time.*

From there on we get down to the business of really making money. The next three chapters start you on your way. They detail how to find ideas that fit your money needs—how to make sure each idea is something you can really do—how to give each a unique flair—how to decide which wealth-building projects are for you, and how to test them.

Chapters 7 through 12 are the money do-it chapters. They detail how to develop your money-making ideas—how to market and promote them—exactly where to get the cash to start in the

5

first place—how to manage effectively, and how to use other people to rocket yourself to riches.

The final chapters deal with increasing your wealth. They show you how to expand and pyramid, how to keep simple records and make them propel you to a fortune, and exactly how to re-invest for even more profits.

Throughout the book you'll find extensive sources of information, tables and charts to help you gauge your progress, plus concrete examples and illustrations that make your own spare-time fortune-making practical.

Of course, what is a fortune to one reader may not necessarily be a fortune to another, but in this book we use fortune to mean an income or dollar amount several times greater than what a person was originally earning before he started applying the principles of spare-time moneymaking.

The emphasis throughout is on steps to positive action so you can easily go from where you are right now to a big-money income.

Duane G. Newcomb

Contents

Check these money-making areas · How to come up with money-making ideas · Make sure each final idea is something you can do · Now add a flare to each · Make sure each idea is really money-oriented · Checking on Chapter 4

Check the idea against what you can actually do · Make sure it's practical · Compare your idea to others that are making money · Check the idea against your skill list · Decide if it feels right for you · How to analyze the project with your needs in mind · Use a good, better, best big money elimination system · Checking on Chapter 5

Ask for other people's opinions · Compare what you want to do with similar businesses · Try a one "ad" test run · How to set up a sample product or idea test · How to "consumer test" your idea · How to run a one magazine new product test · Try the trade show test · Use this magic money potential formula to get rich fast · Use your own judgment · Checking on Chapter 6

Lay out a complete action plan · List everything you need · How to line up your sources of supply · Use the brains and talent of all potential suppliers · How to get help from the government · Find a similar project and go through step by step · Look at all angles in the beginning · Get an idea of cost · How to actually get started with your project · Checking on Chapter 7

How to decide which channels are for you · Automatic selling tools that will propel you to a big money income · How to look for big money outlets · How to use classified ads ef-

fectively · How to find potential customers by mail · How to utilize fairs and shows effectively · How to approach large chains · How to develop foreign markets at home · How to use others to help market your product · Checking on Chapter 8

How to make and use news releases effectively · How to make the local press pay off · How to turn television and radio into a gold mine · How to create a splash both locally and nationally · Promote yourself with the people who really count · How to use the phone effectively · How to get others to sell for you · Checking on Chapter 9

Make a list of all possible money sources · Friends and relatives · You can use bank charge cards to get started · How to get money by mail · Start a nickel and dime investment fund · How to get a small investment group together · How to turn your assets into immediate investment money · Checking on Chapter 10

How to see the whole picture · Lay out a "necessary chore" schedule · Check your work effectiveness · How to sort out priorities · How to double your productive powers · How to keep your expenses down · How to manage your profits effectively · How to short-cut details · Checking on Chapter 11

When to put other people in charge · Use experts to increase income · How to recruit people for your fortune making activities · How to supervise others effectively · Make up a written policy · How to get double and triple work · Know when to hire it done · How to get other people to help · How to use the incentive system effectively · Checking on Chapter 12

Spare-Time Fortune Guide

Chapter I

How to Start Toward
Your Spare-Time Fortune

Start Your Fortune Building Today

Everybody today wants and needs money—lots of it. Yet everywhere you turn, the average guy finds himself hamstrung by rising expenses, increased money needs and the desperate realization that he can't let go of his steady paycheck to strike out full-time in search of real riches.

If this is your problem, stop worrying right now—you don't need more time or money, nor do you need to quit your present job. Making big money, after all, is a state of mind, actionized toward success. All you have to do to get your share is to decide you want wealth, lay out a concrete plan and start toward it—on a concise step-by-step program that zooms you along to big money.

Decide What You Want—
Actually Lay Out A Plan

Every big fortune today started with a decision to get that fortune. If you expect to make big money in your spare time, you must decide to go after it.

Napoleon Hill, in his book *Think And Grow Rich* (The Ralston Society, 1948), stresses these six money-making steps:

(1) Fix the exact amount of money you desire in your mind—be extremely definite in the amount.

(2) Determine what you intend to do for this money.

(3) Establish a definite date when you intend to possess the money.

(4) Create a definite plan and begin immediately to put this into action (ready or not).

(5) Write out a clear, concise statement of the amount of money you want, name the time limit, state what you intend to do and describe your plan.

(6) Read your written statement twice daily.

Probably the most important step here is to actually lay out a working plan. In the beginning, of course, you won't have any idea how you're going to get there.

How To See The Big Money Possibilities Everywhere

There's money everywhere, but most people fail to get the most out of their plan because they don't concentrate on making money. They may be interested in doing a good job—developing better equipment, inventing new ways of doing things—benefiting other people or simply enjoying life. But unfortunately that isn't enough. To make money—really big money—you must concentrate on money, not on the job itself.

A recent study of top U.S. millionaires showed they all had one common trait. Every last one wanted to make money for money's sake. Although they were involved in dozens of different industries from oil to timber, they were more interested in making money than in doing anything else. Money to them had become an intense burning desire. Although you may not set your sight on $100,000,000—if making money is important, then take a hint from these millionaires and consider everything in terms of just how much you can make out of it.

How does this work? Let's see!

One bright young government worker, whose chief goal is making money, realized there's lots of extra cash around. But in order to pick up his share, he concentrated on money itself and not the details of the job.

First, he began a part-time rug cleaning service on Saturdays, with $200 capital he'd saved from his regular job. These clients he solicited with ads in the yellow pages, newspaper and personal contact. He also carried a line of new carpeting for anyone who might need it.

On the job he looked around carefully, and noted other possible needs. These included: shower repair, interior re-painting, new linoleum and more . . . these he solicited, and (for a fee) turned the actual work over to a company specializing in this type of activity.

For offices, he put out a brochure offering soundproofing, remodeling and lighting by other firms who handle all jobs.

Finally, he carried a line of cleaning products (wall and rug cleaners, etc.) which he offered to anyone who seemed interested.

This businessman also has picked up fees for finding landscaping and maintenance jobs, for redecorating offices, for installing outdoor lighting and a lot more.

In a typical case a $100 cleaning job will net our man $300 to $400 after he's collected all subsidiary fees. In a recent year this "extra" money added up to over $40,000, all for simply being aware of the opportunity—an amount he'd never make if he hadn't concentrated mainly on money.

In another case, Tom Holbrook, a California teacher, woke up one morning to discover his son had been injured and he needed $10,000 to cover expenses.

At this point, Tom was just barely making it financially. Expenses for his family of five had been heavy and he still owed $1500 on a loan he'd taken out when his wife was operated on two years before. This last blow was almost too much. And he had no idea where this money would come from.

But since Tom had already discussed going to work part-time for a local insurance broker, Tom decided to keep an eye out for possibilities the next day or two.

That afternoon a fellow teacher mentioned he was going to need some additional insurance soon. Seeing an opportunity, Tom said: "Let me provide it for you." Later, when talking to the principal about some new bleachers, Tom immediately saw another opportunity and asked if he could provide some special insurance. The result—another sale. This kept up throughout the day and although he had never been in the insurance business before, he lined up twelve prospects in two days. All of these he presented to the surprised broker, who immediately put him to work on a whole new list of prospects. Miraculously, almost overnight, the $10,000 was within his grasp.

You, of course, don't have to use these methods, but you must start getting a "nose" for money and realize you can make it at every turn if you learn to recognize which opportunities are money-making ones.

Think Money At All Times

The secret, then, is to look for money-making opportunities every minute of every day—at work, at lunch, at meetings, in the car, at home, at a school board meeting, at a political rally—everywhere. Continually ask yourself: "How can I make money from what's going on around me right now?"

Suppose, for instance, you've just bought a small truck and expect to make some money in your spare time by hauling. One of your fellow workers says he's moving next week and hates to hire a mover—immediately, you offer to either do it, or to rent him your truck . . . a friend tells you that he has ten fruit trees with the fruit spoiling on the trees because nobody wants it—a light goes on—you offer him a share of the profits if he will pick the fruit, use your truck and sell it by the roadside on weekends . . . your boss mentions that the company is thinking of leasing an extra truck—you ask him if he'd like yours . . . a neighbor says she and her husband know where they can get sand for some flower beds, but are hesitant about renting a truck. You offer to get it for her at a reduced rate.

While these examples seem elementary, very few people think this way. To take advantage of this method, you must get money-oriented and let everything and everybody clue you in.

Getting Profit-Oriented Can Make You Rich

Milton Littleton (a full-time pharmaceutical salesman) did a terrific mail order business, selling pine cone novelties that he, himself, had invented. The first year he grossed $10,000, the second $40,000, the third $60,000 and the fourth he went broke. The reason—Milton wasn't a businessman. While his business continued to grow, he added extra expenses at an even faster rate. For instance, on the advice of his two employees, he doubled his office size, installed fancy furniture, ordered a $1,000 photocopier, put in bottled water, hired a receptionist, bought five trucks, rented a 6,000 sq. ft. warehouse, installed a new conveyor system, a cone drier, extra storage racks and a special lighting system.

When added to his other expenses, his total monthly payments, salaries and fixed expenses exceeded $10,000 a month—$800 a month more than he expected to take in during the entire fourth year.

Milton could have avoided this easily by keeping his eye on the profits and simply not letting his expenses cut into the amount needed to keep growing.

In one unusual study of fifteen advertising companies, the ones who made outstanding success were the ones that figured out how much profit they must make first, added up all possible expenses, and charged accordingly. In addition, all the way through every project, they kept their eye on profit to make sure it didn't get eaten away by expenses.

On the other hand, those who were just making it thought mainly in terms of getting the job done—not in how much profit they were going to make.

As you begin, then, it won't be enough to just think money— you will also have to concentrate on how much money you have left over after you've done everything else.

Start Small—Grow Big Fast

On your way to a spare-time fortune, it doesn't matter where you start. The trick is to begin making money from some enterprise and push on from there. Begin small, if you like, by painting numbers on curbs in your spare time (a $10 investment), by setting up a spare-time newspaper crew (a $160 investment), by starting a part-time mail order home canned jam and jelly business (a $150 investment), or anything else. If you have the capital, you can go into business in real style. But you don't need a lot of money to make a spare-time fortune. In fact, it's far better to put as little money into your business as possible and make it pay for itself as you go along. The point simply is, it doesn't matter where you start, but *you must start*.

Begin wherever it's easy and practical. Then, using the techniques outlined in this book, start aiming toward really big money.

Set Up A Regular Big Money Work Schedule

Regular schedules are an important tool, and the less time you have to devote to your money-making activities, the more important they become.

You'll find there is a certain magic about regularity. Even with only an hour a day, you can create an empire. In fact, the less time you have available, the more you're going to make that time really count.

The secret is to simply set aside the same time every day. Decide how much you can devote to your project—thirty minutes, an hour, two hours—then start and finish at the same time.

If you don't believe this is important, try starting at different times haphazardly, or simply let a day or two lapse between work periods.

In the beginning, you will want mainly to work out your goals—next, start looking for ideas—then begin implementing them.

A Fast Action Plan For Automatic Success

As you progress, you'll find it's important not to keep adding new ideas, but to actually put the ideas you have into action. To do this, you'll need some sort of a system.

Here are your steps:

Decide what kind of skills you have—come up with an idea—sort out those projects, decide on one, test it, develop it, find a market for it, promote it, manage it and pyramid it.

Now, lay these steps out on a piece of paper—actually write them down—leave enough space under each so you can make notes on exactly how you want to proceed. For instance, under *ideas*, you might jot down the following:

> Go through the newspaper every night and write down anything
> that looks interesting. Go to the library and browse—go through
> the telephone yellow pages, looking for interesting business
> ideas—list all ideas and eliminate the poorest ones.

When you're writing down your plans, put in as many *how-to* details as possible. This attention is what's going to make your plans practical. At this point, don't do any actual work—simply get it down on paper.

At the same time you're making basic plans, also start accumulating as much practical information as possible.

Tom Henshaw was extremely serious about starting a small business that would put his family on easy street. He laid out a plan, going into great detail about what he wanted to do, then started writing for information. He contacted the Department of Commerce, the Small Business Administration, the Business Department of his local college, and several others. When ready to begin he had a great deal of information on how to handle his inventory, how to manage his business, how to advertise, and other essentials. Because he'd done this groundwork well, Tom now has an automatic income of $35,000 a year and a business that practically runs itself.

Now, let's get started:

(1) Write to the Small Business Administration, Washington, D.C. and ask for any useful pamphlets or information.

(2) Go to your library and look up the government agencies in the *United States Government Organization Manual* which might pertain to what you're trying to do. Write to these and ask for anything they might have which could help you.

(3) Write to the Superintendent of Documents, U.S. Government Printing Office, Washington, D.C. 20402 and ask to receive the list of *Selected U.S. Government Publications*. When these start coming in, pore over them and send for anything useful.

Step-By-Step To Your Own Personal Fortune

The way to actionize your work plan is to start with the first step and simply make a commitment that you must follow through. George Lionel, for instance, was getting extremely tired of his low-paying factory job. An accident the year before had taken a good portion of his savings, and living expenses were now eating up the rest. At the moment he desperately needed money for food, clothing and rent, with no idea where it would come from. Then suddenly he got a bright idea—he'd open a children's used clothing store.

For this he needed money, a store, children's clothes, advertising and more. Knowing that the way to actionize himself was to make a commitment, he visited his local bank and authorized them to take $30 out of his bank account every month. This forced him to accumulate the money.

When he had $500, he signed a lease for a small building at $150 a month—this forced him to take the next step. George then took out an ad offering to buy children's used clothes—this forced him to actually buy. From this point on, he kept committing himself to things which forced him on.

Today, he owns a string of stores and makes a personal income of a little over $75,000 a year.

You, too, can follow George Lionel's example. Start by making a written commitment to yourself, write down what you're going to do and how you're going to do it, then start making commitments that force you on to the next step. Here are a few:

1. Sign up for a course.
2. Authorize your bank to take money out of your checking account.
3. Make an appointment with someone who can help you.
4. Order some supplies.
5. Take out an ad.

These are just a few—as we go along in this book, we'll give you dozens of others.

Checking On Chapter 1

Start heading for big money immediately. Every fortune started with a decision; make yours now.

Have a plan. Most experts find the fastest way to any goal is to lay out a written plan of action this way:

A. Decide what you want.
B. Decide in broad terms how you'll go about it.
C. Establish a completion date.

Think money. Money is everywhere. The secret is to look for the money possibilities in everything, every step of the way.

Lay out a system. Money-making means laying out on a piece of paper, in a general way:

A. The skills you intend to use.
B. The ideas you have.
C. The projects you want to work on.
D. Your test ideas.
E. The development possibilities.

F. Marketing ideas.

G. Management and expansion possibilities.

It also means setting up a definite time schedule and accumulating as much information as possible in the beginning stages. Start actionizing now!

The only way to start is to make some sort of a commitment, then follow through.

Chapter 2

How to Take Stock of
Your Money-Making Skills

You can make money the easy way or the hard way. Some people seem to zoom to riches without effort, while others strain and struggle and never seem to get anywhere. The basic secret is that the people who get ahead easily are the ones who utilize their natural skills—to put them on the track toward big money.

It's primarily a matter of lining up your best-ability-skills with the most promising activities, then letting both of them work for you.

Ben Hamilton, for instance, made friends easily. People liked, trusted and respected him. After college, Ben went directly into teaching.

Using his skills, he acquired many friends and rose quickly to high school principal at a salary of $15,000 a year. Ben, however, had a problem. He enjoyed the good things in life just a little bit too much: his home was just a little too expensive, the payments on his car were more than he could really afford, and he and his family took elaborate summer vacations that took almost the rest of the year to pay for. Now he was faced with the prospect of having to come up with $10,000 to $15,000 extra in the next few years to put his two teenage daughters through college. It was at this point that Ben took stock of himself and realized that while he was utilizing his skills effectively, they weren't making him much money. On closer examination, he also realized that utilizing natural skills to make big money required two things:

(1) The skills themselves, and

(2) Putting them to work on activities that lead directly to big money.

As a result, Ben resigned the dead-end job that was holding him back from making real money and started selling insurance. Utilizing the same ability with people that had been an asset in his school job, he soon discovered he was a natural insurance salesman. At the end of the first year he made $16,000, $32,000 the second, and the third, almost $75,000. Ben put two basic money-making factors together—his natural skill and the right kind of activity. Kept apart, they were keeping him back—brought together they really zoomed him along, bringing in big money at every turn.

This example, of course, is too simple to apply to everyone, yet it serves to illustrate the point that you must utilize your natural skills on activities that can lead directly to money.

Here are a few others—an underpaid cook, making $125 a week in a local restaurant, eventually made $60,000 a year selling prize preserves by mail—a hard-working expert mechanic, on a modest $800 a month salary, zoomed to $5000 a month when he started a school to train more mechanics—a hard-pressed housewife, who enjoyed finding out who a person's relatives were, rocketed to $50,000 a year by tracing the history of a family name like Wells or Rogers, then selling that history to people with the name of Wells or Rogers all over the United States—all examples of taking a natural skill and putting it on a direct money track.

As we proceed in this book, we will continually talk about how to get on the money track. First, however, we must take stock of our own skill abilities.

Zoom To Riches On Your Fortune-Making Skills

We've been talking about the fact that it's necessary to pick activities that have good money-making potential. Now, let's reverse that and say it's extremely important to fit your skills first to your fortune-making. That is, don't strike out toward money by doing something for which you have no natural ability. You'll progress a lot faster and be a lot happier if you do things which come easily to you.

Bill Allen, for instance, was energetic, extremely ambitious, and determined to make money. Knowing he could make big money selling, he immediately took a commission job selling heavy equipment in California. During the first year, Bill barely eked out a living. His children's dental work kept him broke and expensive repairs on his car threatened to send him deep into bankruptcy. Desperate, he bought a lot of small trees from a local nursery for $50, packaged them in fancy milk containers, set them up attractively at a local fair auction, and sold his entire stock within three hours.

Two months later, utilizing only his evenings, Bill's income exceeded $5,000 a month, with 25 people selling trees for him all over the state.

The reason? Bill's artistic and creative talents helped him design packages and booths that really appealed to people. This was correct utilization of his skill—the other kind of selling wasn't.

Take Stock Of Your Success Skills

The first thing you must do is to decide exactly what your skills are. In the beginning, these will be vague. But, by using the skill-ability chart on p. 35, you can come up with a fairly accurate appraisal. Simply go over each one and try to decide where you fall. Then, look over the list of activities provided and see which your "skill-abilities" seem to match. This chart is a generalization of an extremely good method of matching skills and abilities to types of work. While it isn't as accurate as a battery of tests, it will give you a gauge to work against.

How To Fit Your Skills To
Particular Money-Making Areas

Once you know your abilities and the activities you're suited for, you can estimate, in a general way, your chances for success in particular areas. The trick, of course, is to break down those things which you're thinking about doing into their components and see how you stack up. Suppose, for instance, you decide you'd like to try to collect delinquent accounts for local businessmen.

First, look at the steps. If you want to run this into a large business, it means starting with a one-man operation, then stepping up to one in which you're supervising several employees.

Now, let's see what your chances are. First, you'll need the initiative (business initiative) to get going and be a self-starter. Second, you'll need to be a salesman (general sales), to convince your businessmen customers in the first place. Third, you must be able to make face to face contacts easily (people-centered personality). Finally, you'll need the ability to recruit and handle people (management).

Now, look at how you rated yourself on these items and see how you stack up. If they're fairly weak, consider something else. If medium, you should be strongly motivated before proceeding. If strong, then go ahead.

Next, assuming you have the skill to make an overall success, look at the other things you'll be doing: you'll need to actually make calls demanding money—you'll need to set up a system of letters (clerical)—you'll need to keep books (bookkeeping)—you'll need to go to small claims court, and more. Again, list the skills and see how you measure up. You may well be low in some of these, since they're often in direct contrast to your dominant needs. Don't worry about it. Simply make a mental note that you'll need to work harder in these areas, or hire someone who can do it for you.

Chart Your Big Money Skills

From the overall chart, you can see what types of activities fit you best. Now make up your own personal chart, as shown here. Mark your ratings in all sixteen areas. Then list the types of work that seem to fit you best. This will give you a tool with which to work as you go through the rest of the book, learning how to propel yourself to riches in your spare time.

How To Actually Put Your
Skills To Work

The biggest problem most of us have is going from skills to actual use, and from there to big money. The secret, of course, is to select those areas that take advantage of the skills you do have.

Suppose, for instance, one of your dominant skills is writing, and you plan an advertising service for small businesses. First, look over the field—find the best ads you can and copy them, substituting your own product. Take these down to a fast print service ($3.50 a hundred) and make up samples so you'll have something to actually show.

Next, go around and solicit businessmen. Remember, you're there to fill a need. Ask him what his advertising needs are—tell him you'll go home, think over his problems, and come back with some ideas.

At home, try to decide how you can best serve his needs. Make up sample ads, using the best examples you can find, then go back and present your product. The secret, then, in anything, is to take your dominant skill in whatever activity you decide on, and copy the examples of the very best in the field.

Make yourself a notebook of what they're doing—then put your own skill to work to turn out a job that's as good or better. This step is extremely important if you intend to rocket yourself to success.

How To Multiply Your Income From
One Business—And Watch It Grow!

By using your dominant skills effectively, you can propel yourself a long way. But that's not enough. You've got to use the interest of your skills. That is, you must use your skills in such a way that the effects multiply themselves.

Bob Henderson, for instance, had been an entertainer, liked to write, and had a great gift of gab. Unfortunately, the small night club he'd been working in closed and he wound up in a low-paying hectic job driving a bus in a large city. He was also forced to sell his house and move into a crowded apartment. His children were in need of new clothes and his old run-down car threatened to give up at any moment. Bob was certainly down, but he knew that with just a little imagination he could bounce back big. On one of his days off, he approached a weekly newspaper publisher in another city with the idea that he would go out and sell ads to create an entire "entertainment section" within his own column. The publisher was hesitant but decided to give it a try. The first week Bob sold eight ads and filled part of a page. The next week he sold 16 and the following week 48. By the end of the second month he had his own four-page section and was packing away almost $250 a week.

At this point Bob decided to apply just a little more of his imagination. He knew he was limited to the number of ads he himself could sell. He also knew the only way he could really expand was to multiply himself—that is, to sell what he was already doing many times. Bob then took his original columns to a radio station and sold the manager on doing the very same thing on the air, ten minutes every week.

After that, he started a monthly entertainment brochure sent out to area residents and placed in motel rooms. Again, this simply incorporated the best material from his columns and ads from his original contacts. As Bob became more successful (to the tune of $16,000 a year in his spare time), he expanded his advertisers—but still carbon-copied his newspaper material, turning it many ways to expand his income and use his talents without having to do something new every time. He was soon able to quit his bus driving job with an income that made his former one look like peanuts.

This is a good example of letting your money-making skills multiply your income. You, too, can do this effectively. Simply ask yourself how you can reach additional markets—with what you're already doing. What you offer should be identical (or almost so) to what you're doing now. The differences are the market or audience—and (like Bob), the package you present it in.

This will take a little imagination, but it's well worth the time you'll spend.

The Positive Path To Riches

Unfortunately, in our quest toward riches, all of us are going to run into roadblocks. What we want to do here is to help you find the shortest path to great wealth—and eliminate all obstacles along the way. The problem in the beginning, however, is to recognize what you're poor at, and to minimize the harmful effects.

Bill Borden of Kansas City, for example, was an excellent salesman. However, he picked a food freezer plan to sell that required phone solicitation. After a few calls, Bill discovered he was terrified of making appointments over the phone.

The terror he felt was unreasonable, yet he couldn't seem to cope with it. He knew, however, that he had to lick this problem. His solution was to make ten calls that didn't count—every day for two weeks.

When it wasn't important it didn't seem to matter, and the calls went without a hitch. After getting himself in the habit for two weeks, Bill found he could continue easily and handle the authentic prospects without any trouble. As a result his income soon zoomed to almost $50,000 a year.

This, of course, isn't the only answer. Here are some of the other solutions to overcome deficiencies:

Practice until you're perfect—like Bill, you can do the chore without pressure until it becomes a habit.

Substitute activities for something you can do well—actually, if Bill found he couldn't overcome his telephone sales problem, he could have tried making door-to-door appointments. Although this does not overcome the problem, it effectively goes around it.

Eliminate it entirely—if you're not good at an activity, sometimes you can get around it by eliminating the activity itself. In Bill's case, he might simply have eliminated the telephone appointment stage and gone directly to the prospect's house. This might have worked fine for him, or it might not—you'll have to find out for yourself.

Pick up the additional knowledge or skill you need to overcome the problem—in some cases your problem may be simply that you don't have the necessary knowledge. For instance, suppose you need bookkeeping for a certain phase of your business and you just don't have it. The only way you're going to acquire this is to get a book out of the library, or take a course and actually pick up the knowledge—don't kid yourself and try to skip it. Recognize that a thorough grounding is important. This, of course, doesn't apply to the skill-abilities in the chart, since these primarily are personality qualities that are difficult to change or acquire. But it does apply to acquirable abilities and knowledge.

Use a mind conditioning approach—some deficiencies can be approached this way. For instance, suppose you have a hard time meeting people. Sometimes it's simply a problem of self-image. In Maxwell Maltz's book *Psycho-Cybernetics* he explains that it's possible to pick up this experience synthetically. He recommends that you see yourself meeting people for thirty minutes a day for 21 days—that is, you imagine yourself meeting them, everybody smiles, you feel relaxed and confident, and everything goes well.

You then proceed to simply do what you have to do—you do not use will power, but you let your subconscious take over and do the work for you. Naturally, you can't use this technique on everything—but sometimes personality habits can be changed.

Start Building Money-Making Power Today!

As you go along building your spare-time fortune, you will need new knowledge skills from time to time. The time to start thinking about them is right now. Maybe today it's enough to be industrious. But you'll find, as you get more and more successful, that it is extremely helpful to become: (1) *proficient at writing skills* so you can communicate with others effectively on paper, (2) *to develop your face-to-face communication skills,* and (3) *your vocabulary skills* with others.

As you go along, pick those items which you think you're going to need in the near future.

Suppose, for instance, your projects demand a great deal of selling. You may decide you need to know how to get along with people better. The first step, take out a book—a good one is *How To Make Friends and Influence People* by Dale Carnegie. This may be all you need; if not, then you might also want to take the Dale Carnegie course or similar courses, in person (check your phone book for addresses).

How To Evaluate Your Skill Utilization

It's fine to match skills to projects, but you've got to also make sure that you utilize these skills efficiently.

Thomas Dale, for instance, at one time had been a good writer and a college Journalism major. When he first started his small part-time business, however, he didn't really need this skill.

Later, when he began writing letters and memos, he tended to be extremely wordy. People had a hard time reading through what he wrote and often misunderstood it when they did. Although Tom had the skill needed in this case, he under-utilized it completely.

To avoid this, rate yourself. Chart the work-skills you're using and rate them *poor, fair, good, excellent.* Simply ask yourself (for instance) if you meet people as well as you should—are you doing a good writing job—do you make full use of your time and more. You probably don't need to do anything more with the skills rated good and excellent, but you should start giving special attention now to the others.

Checking On Chapter 2

1. To do your best you must find what skills you're proficient at, and put them to work on activities that lead directly to big money.
2. Try to fit skills to your project—slight adjustments can make a big difference.
3. Take stock of your skill abilities by checking them carefully on the chart listed here. The primary skill abilities are:
   a. People-Centered Personality
   b. Self-Centered Personality
   c. Idea Ability
   d. Record Keeping Ability
   e. Fact Fitting Ability
   f. The Three Dimension Factor
   g. Hand and Finger Speed
   h. Small Tool Handling Ability
   i. Observation
   j. Pattern Memory
   k. Music Memory
   l. Number Memory
   m. Decorating Ability
   n. Energy
   o. The Get There Factor
4. Fit your skills to money-making areas by breaking down your project steps—then see if what you do well fits.
5. Put your skills to work by finding the best examples available, then copying them in the beginning—try to make yours better than the models you're using.
6. Multiply what you're doing by finding different markets for it, and by changing the approach.
7. Overcome your deficiencies by using these methods:
   a. *Practice till perfect* on an activity that doesn't count.
   b. *Substitute activities*—replace something you don't do well with something you do.
   c. *Eliminate that step entirely.*
   d. *Pick up needed skills or knowledge.*
   e. *Use mind conditioning.*
8. Acquire knowledge you need for future activities—you can get this from either books or courses.
9. Evaluate how you're putting the skills you do have into practice. Rate what you're doing as *excellent, good, fair, poor*—make a special effort to correct the ones you do poorly.

Skill Ability Chart

**Write down your own rating number
(from 1 to 5) for each of these skill-abilities
on a separate sheet of paper.**

PEOPLE-CENTERED PERSONALITY––The extent to which you like to work with others.

5. Outgoing–people around, a real joiner, surrounded by people, many friends, seldom get hurt feelings, everybody likes you.
4. Talker–goes out of way to be with people, very friendly.
3. Enjoys having people around–moderately friendly.
2. Likes people–moderate talker, mostly likes to work with others, but sometimes would prefer to do things alone.
1. Can take people or leave them–still on outgoing side, but enjoys working alone almost as much as working with others.

SELF-CENTERED PERSONALITY––The extent to which you enjoy working alone.

5. Don't really like being with people–much prefer to work alone and spend hours doing it–disturbed by slights and rebuffs, disturbed by human frailties–think of yourself a lot, want to be left alone.
4. You are content being by yourself–you often spend considerable time working out things in your own mind.
3. You can work by yourself–sometimes you'd just as soon be and work with others–you don't mind long hours by yourself, but sometimes you simply need to get away from this and talk to other people.
2. Can do isolated jobs, but would prefer not to–are a fairly good talker, but sometimes like to be alone.
1. Still would rather work alone than with others–but can basically take people or leave them alone–sometimes outgoing, sometimes a little turned in.

IDEA ABILITY––The measure of how easily ideas come to you.

5. You get a continuous flow of ideas about everything. If something goes wrong, you have twenty ideas how to fix it. You also have a wild imagination.
4. You are a good idea man. You like to create things; you have a good imagination, but not wild.

3. You would rather deal with ideas than have to work them out—they come easily, but you want to stop when it comes to putting them into practice. Ideas don't flow out of you constantly, however. (You get ideas, but they don't flow out of you like water—you have to work to come up with different ways of doing things.)

2. You don't get ideas too easily—you have to work on it—you would rather take someone else's idea than dream up some of your own.

1. You seldom have an original idea. Everything you do belongs to someone else—those ideas you put into use came from somewhere else.

RECORD KEEPING ABILITY—Measures your ability to do systematic paperwork, filing, etc.

5. You'd rather file, you keep records easily, efficiently and in good order—you have good ability at alphabetizing and it comes easily—you would probably rather do these things than most others.

4. You're good at columns of figures, bookkeeping, filing, and keeping records; however, you also like many other things.

3. You have some difficulty keeping records—you don't like to file, and you have difficulty with systematic work with numbers.

2. You can keep records and do paperwork, but it doesn't come easily—frequently your records get out of order, but you don't really care for filing and sometimes you misfile.

1. Never ask you to keep records—you can't do it—and any kind of systematic paperwork drives you up the wall.

FACT FITTING ABILITY—This measures your ability to take a lot of isolated facts, put them into sequence and come to a conclusion.

5. You have the ability to pick up facts from everywhere, fit them all together and come up with an answer. You can see their relationship—even though you may find these facts in many isolated spots.

4. You're pretty good at putting things together, from everywhere, to form a conclusion. It isn't easy for you, but it isn't hard either.

3. You can put information together to form a conclusion, but it must be fairly obvious—often isolated pieces of informa-

tion don't make much sense to you and you can't see the relationship.

2. If people give you a lot of facts and ask you what you make out of it, you have a hard time—you can give them an answer, but you have a hard time at it.

1. You can't form a conclusion at all from a series of related information—you just don't see the relationship at all.

THE THREE DIMENSION FACTOR——Measures your ability to think in three dimensions.

5. Can visualize things in any position and any combination—can take a number of physical things, turn them around and know exactly how they'll fit together in a situation (for instance, you can see exactly how a whole room full of furniture would look moved into a different room, and put in a different position).

4. You are good at thinking in three dimensions. You do well on tests where you have to move three dimensional objects around. However, you do have to strain sometimes to visualize these things.

3. You can see in three dimensions—you can, for instance, turn things different ways and imagine what they'd look like—but you have to work with it.

2. It's possible for you to see in three dimensions—but you have difficulty. On a test, where you must turn three dimensional objects a number of ways, you miss many of them.

1. You can't visualize anything but what's there—try to imagine it in any other position or in any other combination, and you fail.

HAND AND FINGER SPEED——This measures the nimbleness of your fingers and hands (quickness).

5. You are extremely quick with your hands. You can do jobs with your hands rapidly. If you have to pick up a bunch of marbles with other people, you get there first with the most.

4. You'll do jobs with your hands faster than many people, but you aren't a whiz either, just extra good.

3. You are only moderately rapid and quick with your hands. If you have to fold papers with others, you do as well as anybody else, but no better.

2. You can do things well with your hands but you aren't rapid—you're systematic and plodding with them.

1. You have terrible manual dexterity. You always come in last in a test of speed at picking things up.

SMALL TOOL HANDLING ABILITY——This measures the ability to work well with small tools.

5. You like to work in detail with your hands. You can easily pick up small things with tweezers and move them around —working in a watch for hours is just your meat— and you are quite skillful at this kind of detail—you can easily be a master craftsman.

4. You enjoy building models. You can take a watch apart and put it back together easily. However, you'd never call yourself a master craftsman.

3. You can build models and work with your hands. You have about average ability in working with detail. You can repair a watch with small tools, but you fumble a lot.

2. You can do some detailed things with your hands, but you'd rather not—it's hard and you don't like it.

1. Trying to work with small tools drives you up the wall—you hate it. You get extremely nervous even trying to put a few screws in a wall.

OBSERVATION——This measures your ability to notice things and retain details.

5. You look at a window of 50 or 60 items, walk down the street and you can recall them perfectly. You also notice the color, shape, size and how they relate to each other. If a friend comes by that night, you can tell him what color and kind of socks, shirt, pants, shoes he had on, and all other details.

4. You're good at noticing and recall—you can, after leaving a doctor's waiting room, recall everyone there. You couldn't recall 50 or 60 things, but you do all right.

3. You have about average ability to notice and retain things— if we gave you a number of advertising trademarks and asked you what products they went to, you could pick up some of them, but not all.

2. You don't notice and retain too well. You're more preoccupied with yourself and things around you. If you sat down

in a room for five minutes, then walked away, you probably couldn't list 25 percent of the things in the room.

1. You don't observe or retain much of anything. Your wife or husband could walk in with a whole new outfit, and you wouldn't know the difference. In addition, five minutes later you couldn't tell them what they had on.

PATTERN MEMORY——Measures your ability to retain patterns and designs well.

5. You can see a pattern or design and copy it perfectly in every detail.

4. You are good at retaining and copying design. You don't do it rapidly and quickly, but you're pretty good at it nevertheless.

3. Just medium ability to retain a design. When trying to reproduce a design on paper, you will make some mistakes—it will only be moderately good.

2. Can manage to reproduce a design so you can recognize it, but that's about all.

1. Cannot retain designs at all. No ability to reproduce a design on paper—it is always a disaster.

MUSIC MEMORY——Test ability to distinguish and remember sounds as well as separate notes.

5. Can distinguish sounds well—are good at telling minute differences in notes—love music, extra special talent.

4. You can remember music well, enjoy it, and go around humming and singing—you are a good musician.

3. You can distinguish sounds and tell differences in notes but not well—you also can take music or leave it alone.

2. You have a tendency to be sharp or flat when you sing—you can't remember songs, or get them right when you try.

1. You are tone deaf. Every attempt to sing is a disaster.

NUMBER MEMORY——Tests your ability to remember columns and numbers.

5. You can remember all sorts of telephone numbers—you almost have a photographic memory for figures—give you ten numbers at once and you'll remember them easily.

4. You can remember numbers well—you can't reel off ten telephone numbers at one time, but you do all right just the same.

3. You can remember a few selected telephone numbers—but you forget as many as you remember.

2. You can remember only a few numbers, and sometimes you forget those.

1. Can't retain numbers at all—have a hard time remembering your own telephone number, and you often forget that.

DECORATING ABILITY—Measures the ability to tell if patterns and combinations are eye pleasing.

5. You are a natural born decorator—everything you touch you add an aesthetic touch to—you understand color well and know exactly what goes with what.

4. You like to decorate—you're better than average—you understand how things relate to each other, and you can easily put together eye-pleasing combinations.

3. You can arrange a room so it's eye-pleasing, but you're not the world's best—you do all right, however.

2. Most of your design attempts end up being just barely acceptable—you just aren't very good at it.

1. You have no sense of what pleases the eye whatsoever—any attempt to decorate ends up a disaster.

ENERGY——Measures the amount of energy you have to put into projects.

5. You're always bustling around, have a lot of drive, have dozens of projects going—hate to quit and love to work long hours. Your energy literally drives you ahead.

4. Your drive is good—you can spend long hours without tiring too much, but your energy doesn't drive you—you control it.

3. You have about as much energy as anyone else—you, however, want to quit at quitting time and do something else.

2. You have low energy—you put off projects if you can—and you have only one thing going at a time so you won't tax yourself.

1. You have little energy—you don't like to start new projects—too much effort.

THE GET THERE FACTOR——This measures how good you are at setting a goal and continuing to work until you get there.

5. You continually set long-range goals, you don't like to do anything that isn't on your way to the goal—and you

absolutely won't give up until you get there.

4. You set goals well, and you're persistent. However, if you have failure after failure, you may give up before getting there.

3. You sometimes set goals, but they're seldom long-range. For instance, you would seldom say I'm going to strive to be President of the company in ten years—in addition, if you don't make it to your goal, it really doesn't make that much difference—you can go in another direction.

2. You set goals once in a while. They seldom would take over a week or two to complete. If you have to sustain interest in something over that time, you don't really care about it.

1. You never set goals. You simply live from moment to moment—you also have no persistence. If something gets in your way, you stop immediately.

APPLICATION ABILITY——This measures your ability to start with general principles and to figure out how they apply to particular problems.

5. You can take a general principle (such as the law of gravity) and you can understand how it applies to every situation.

4. You can take general principles and apply them in most cases—once in a while, however, individual situations leave you puzzled.

3. You can take general principles and apply them the majority of the time.

2. You understand the principle, but can seldom apply this to particular problems.

1. You do not understand the principle in the first place, and can't apply it to problems.

Skill Ability Ratings Needed For Success In
The Following Fields

ACTIVITY	Advertising	Assembling small things	Bookkeeping & Clerical	Business Initiative	Construction Carpentry Plumbing	Contracting cost accounting	Crafts	Designing houses	Diagnosis
PEOPLE CENTERED PERSONALITY	3+							3+ or above	
SELF CENTERED PERSONALITY							3+		2+
IDEA ABILITY	3+	2 −	3 − or below	2+	3 or below	3 or below	3+	3 or above	2 −
RECORD KEEPING ABILITY		2 −	4 or above		3 or below	3+ or above		3+ or above	
FACT FITTING ABILITY			3 − or below						
THE THREE DIMENSION FACTOR	2 −	2+	3 − or below	2+	4 or above	4 or above	3+	4 or above	3+
HAND AND FINGER SPEED									
SMALL TOOL HANDLING ABILITY		3+					3+		
OBSERVATION									
PATTERN MEMORY									
MUSIC MEMORY									
NUMBER MEMORY									
DECORATING ABILITY									
ENERGY	3+					3	2+	3 or above	2+
THE GET THERE FACTOR	3			3+		3	2+	3 or above	2+
APPLICATION ABILITY	3+				3 or below	2 −			3+

ACTIVITY	General Design	General Management	General selling	Insurance	Inspection of Production	Keeping Production going	Lab Work	Managing Production	Making Surveys
PEOPLE CENTERED PERSONALITY		2	3	2 or above		3+		2	
SELF CENTERED PERSONALITY					1 –				
IDEA ABILITY	3 or above		3+			2 –	2 –		
RECORD KEEPING ABILITY	3 or below	3+		3+ or above		3	3+	3+	3+
FACT FITTING ABILITY				3 or below					
THE THREE DIMENSION FACTOR	4 or above	2 –	2 –	3 or below	2 –		2+	3	3+
HAND AND FINGER SPEED									
SMALL TOOL HANDLING ABILITY							3+		
OBSERVATION					3+				
PATTERN MEMORY									
MUSIC MEMORY									
NUMBER MEMORY						3+			
DECORATING ABILITY									
ENERGY	3	3+	3+	3		3+		2+	
THE GET THERE FACTOR	3	3+	3+	3				2+	
APPLICATION ABILITY	2 –	2 –	2 –					2 –	

ACTIVITY	Music	News-paper work	Nur-sing	Re-search	Stock-room work	Super-vision	Tak-ing Com-plaints	Teach-ing	Tea-ing Mu
PEOPLE CENTERED PERSONALITY	3					2+	2+	3	3
SELF CENTERED PERSONALITY			2+		3+				
IDEA ABILITY		3+				3+	2 −		
RECORD KEEPING ABILITY		2 or below	3+	3+	2+				
FACT FITTING ABILITY				3+			2 −		
THE THREE DIMEN-SION		2 or below		3+		2 −			
HAND AND FINGER SPEED									
SMALL TOOL HAND-LING ABILITY			3 +						
OBSERVATION									
PATTERN MEMORY									
MUSIC MEMORY	3								3+
NUMBER MEMORY					3+				
DECORATING ABILITY								3+	
ENERGY				2+		2	3+		
THE GET THERE FACTOR				2+		3+			
APPLICATION ABILITY		3+		3+		3+	3+	3+	3+

CHART 41

ACTIVITY	Type Setting Etc.	Typing cash register & adding machine	Working with Figures & statistics	Working with musicians	Writing from accumulated facts	Secretarial Work
PEOPLE CENTERED PERSONALITY		1 or 2		3		
SELF CENTERED PERSONALITY		1 or 2			3 or above	2+ or above
IDEA ABILITY	3+	3 or above	3 − or below		3 −	3 − or below
RECORD KEEPING ABILITY	2 or below	3 or below	3+ or above			3 or above
FACT FITTING ABILITY						
THE THREE DIMENSION FACTOR	2 or below	below 3	3 − or below		2 −	below 3
HAND AND FINGER SPEED						
SMALL TOOL HANDLING ABILITY						3 or above
OBSERVATION						
PATTERN MEMORY						
MUSIC MEMORY				3+		
NUMBER MEMORY						
DECORATING ABILITY						
ENERGY		2+	3		3+	
THE GET THERE FACTOR			3		2	
APPLICATION ABILITY	2 or below		3 or above		3+	

Chapter 3

How to Think Like a Millionaire
and Build Your Fortune . . .Fast!

Over his lifetime, Rudolph Johnson had tried various businesses—a hobby shop, a mail order business, a used car lot, a private campground, and even a magazine. All would go well for a few months, then suddenly things would fall apart, and within a short time he'd be bankrupt.

In trying to explain why, Rudolph decided he just wasn't as good as his competition. "They're real sharpies," he rationalized, "I could never expect to compete."

In actuality, Rudolph's problem wasn't lack of ability. His problem was that he "knew" from the beginning he was going to fail—he convinced himself he wasn't as good as anybody else in the business and never would be.

This pre-determined self image programmed Rudolph for failure. This happens to many ambitious people. They're eager, but have such a bad opinion of themselves it literally destroys them. If we intend to succeed big in a spare-time business, one of the first things we must do is build our self image. In this chapter, I'm going to show you how to put your self image on your side and really make it propel you along. It did for Rudolph. Within days of beginning this program, his whole outlook began to change. Shortly afterwards he began a small investment business on a nest egg of $2500. Within a short time his income zoomed, going from a modest $500 a month in the beginning to $600, then $700, and finally over $2000.

He soon moved into a large house in a swanky neighborhood, complete with the best furnishings money could buy and two fancy cars. In addition, his income continued to skyrocket until today it is far greater than anything Rudolph ever dreamed possible. And Rudolph finds it's impossible to fail because he sincerely believes it just can't happen.

Set Yourself A Big Money Goal

Dr. Maxwell Maltz, in his best selling book *Psycho-Cybernetics* (Prentice-Hall, 1960), tells us that discoveries in the science of cybernetics point to the conclusion that the physical brain and nervous system make up what he calls a "servo mechanism" that operates much like a goal-seeking computer. Once you program it effectively, it operates automatically to achieve a goal.

Let's take something simple—say you want to put a basketball through the basket. The first thing you must do is simply throw the ball at the basket. The first time you tried, you were way off. But your brain saw that the ball hit (for instance) low to the left and made a mental correction. Your next shot still hit low, but closer. The brain corrected again, and after awhile you began putting a few through the basket. Later, after much trial and error, the ball went in most of the time and you missed only occasionally.

"The minute you set a goal," Dr. Maltz emphasizes, "the automatic mechanism takes over and begins to correct." This is true of learning a language, learning to dance, trying to pick up a skill, making money, or anything else.

In applying this principle to making money in your spare time, you'll be clumsy at first, but you'll improve with practice. Start toward your money goal the same way you would anything else—by simply picking a goal. (This can be almost anything—$50,000 a year, $100,000 in the bank, a successful business of your own, a fleet of trucks—anything. You decide!!)

Self Image—The Secret To Big Money

John Houston made $6,000 a year selling insurance in a very difficult territory. Because John had done so well, his manager decided to give him a break and move him into a more productive area.

The next year, despite the tremendous opportunity, John made $6000. John was then moved back into another difficult territory where he wasn't expected to do anything. The following year, however, he again made $6000. The whole problem was that John considered himself a $6000 a year man. Because of this he simply couldn't make more.

Fortunately, John's boss finally realized what was happening and decided to do something about it. He immediately called John into the office and explained in great detail how a man's mind could keep him in chains.

John, his boss explained, had an ability far beyond that of a $6000 a year man, but his own self image was tying him in knots. Then the boss put him on a daily program he himself had used some time ago and asked John to try it for just two months. At the end of that time he could make up his own mind.

That's all it took. After the first week John began to feel really successful. Within two months his sales doubled and by the end of the year his income had leaped to over $20,000. Shortly after that John paid off debts that had been hanging over his head for years, had invested in several part-time businesses in addition to his insurance sales job, and was well on his way to a big money income.

It is possible, behavioral scientists have found, to improve not only John's performance, but almost anyone's by building his self image to the point where he is capable of doing almost anything.

The Behavioral Science Center of the Sterling Institute uses this principle quite effectively to produce successful men. In one experimental program, they purposely picked unskilled people, the hard core unemployed and others, then put these people through mental games and problem situations similar to those encountered by successful executives.

In one problem situation in a similar program, for instance, an unskilled worker with a fifth grade education was dressed as an executive, put in charge of an imaginary airline and told to start running it. For the next six days he handled a routine (complete with his own executive secretary and four vice-presidents) similar to one which had confronted a real company president only one month before. He called morning conferences, met emergencies, and handled problems as they arose. On the sixth day the rating team evaluated his performance as 90 percent effective. Additional tests showed he had already begun to acquire many of the traits commonly found in top executives.

This particular individual eventually found a real job in middle management with a small company, jumping his income dramatically. Results obtained with other trainees were similarly striking and showed that people actually became what they thought they were.

The trick, then, is to see yourself as you want to be. One expert urges everyone trying to improve to set aside ten to thirty minutes every day. Then act out the part mentally. See yourself dressed in the proper clothes, talking to important people, giving orders to employees, getting into a fancy car, and anything else that has to do with what you want to become. Pay special attention to the small details. In other words, literally saturate yourself with this idea and keep telling yourself how much you want it. Don't do this haphazardly, either—set aside a period every day and work at it systematically—keep at it until you have transferred your search for big money from something you merely want to do to an intense, burning desire.

Build A Fortune Today— Starting From Scratch!

Success mechanism and success personality actually are two different things. Just what is a success personality, anyway? Primarily, a success personality is somebody who knows he's going to get what he wants out of life, is confident and poised, knows failure is only temporary, and always has his mind on his goal.

It's possible to describe this in other ways. Wilbur Jones bought a California radio station ten years ago with borrowed money, dressed well, knew exactly what he intended to do with his investment, always had a friendly smile, was confident and enthusiastic, and convinced others he was extremely successful. Over the first three years, Wilbur met failure after failure—several firms cancelled major contracts, his employees let him down and business dropped off. At home he found it increasingly difficult to make ends meet, and after a long illness his wife died.

But that didn't discourage Wilbur. He worked up a distinctive musical identification for his station, designed a woodpecker trademark for billboards and bumper stickers, and traded radio spots with newspapers in return for ads to help him get better known.

He then bought two searchlights and offered them free to businesses who advertised new openings on his station. He equipped a travel trailer as a mobile unit and started soliciting "on-the-spot" broadcasts from fairs, shopping centers and businesses, and set himself up a regular schedule to solicit new business.

Whenever he made calls or talked to people he exuded confidence and enthusiasm—Wilbur just knew he was going to succeed. Before long people began to take notice of his station, and within a year he was doing more business than any other station in town. Today, because he never gave up even in the face of failure and personal despair, he is worth millions. *This* is a success personality.

How do you acquire it? It's actually an attitude. Here are some rules for getting there:

(1) Develop a feeling and a nostalgia for the future and always strive toward what you intend to achieve.

(2) Start seeing yourself as a successful person. Begin to visualize yourself as somebody other people envy. Don't degrade yourself, don't think you can't do it, but begin to regard yourself as a super "get-it-done" guy.

(3) Remember only the success—most of us destroy our own self-confidence by remembering past failures and forgetting past successes.

(4) Don't let your mistakes become you. When you make a mistake, tell yourself: "You may have made a mistake, but that mistake is not you, as a person." Don't let the fact, for instance, that you missed a big sale, translate into: "You can't sell well." Just accept it as a fact that in this one instance you didn't do particularly well. This seems to be a hard concept for most people to grasp.

Frank Cox, a mechanical engineer in the aerospace industry, as a young boy got an "F" in Physics. He said to himself: "I failed—I am nothing!" Two days later the teacher called him in and said: "Now, Frank, I know you got an "F," but don't let that influence you. You merely didn't apply yourself—you, as a person, have great talent." Frank thought about that for awhile and realized she was right. He and his failure were not the same thing. The next semester, Frank tackled Physics again and made an "A"—later, in college, he graduated third in his class. Had he convinced himself by his earlier failure that he wasn't much good as a student, the world would have lost an extremely good engineer.

How To Use Enthusiasm As A
Money-Making Tool

If you don't do anything else at this point, get yourself mentally ready to make big money. By all means, start right now generating enthusiasm. This one tool alone will carry you across many obstacles.

Gerald Horton was a salesman earning a meager income with a small farm implement company until he discovered the secret of enthusiasm. From that point on his income zoomed. In his first year in a new territory, selling a rather mediocre farm tractor, he outsold his nearest competitor three to one and made almost $30,000 more than he ever had before.

In trying to analyze his success, his competitor noticed that every time Gerald went out he literally bubbled over with enthusiasm for his product. This enthusiasm was so strong and so convincing that he overcame every objection easily.

How do you learn to be enthusiastic? The best way is to just do it! The Dale Carnegie Courses, however, have a method that works well. Students simply get a rolled up newspaper and bang on a desk or table uncontrollably, until they work themselves up to a high pitch of enthusiasm. This is not anger, but an excitement level that helps overcome any obstacle.

There are other methods. Maxwell Maltz says: "The secret of generating enthusiasm is to let yourself go—in short, break away from your inhibitions."

Here are some rules:

(1) Get excited, don't wonder in advance what you're going to say—just open your mouth and say it.

(2) Make it a habit to *speak louder than usual*—raise your voice, speak rapidly and let people know you really care. If you feel good, say it—don't keep it in, tell it with vigor.

(3) Practice banging a rolled up newspaper with enthusiasm as you make a point.

(4) Be a child again—light up with intense possession, jump about, rave, talk it up like a kid talks up Christmas, let your bars

down and show concern with your subject to the point of childishness.

Maybe all this sounds silly, but it's one of the most important pieces of advice I can give you in this book.

Get That Winning Feeling

What a wonderful thing a winning feeling is. Once you have it, you know you're going where you want to go and, most important, you know you're going to come out on top.

A tennis champion explains it this way:

> "I find that when I'm in peak condition I begin to feel sure I'm going to win. Every move I make is perfect, and my game begins to get better and better. It's like winning is already pre-programmed in my brain. All I have to do is go out there and play. Actually, I think that a winning feeling is everybody's secret of playing winning ball."

There truly is magic in the winning feeling—it can take you straight to your goal without effort, it can overcome obstacles and impossibilities, it can even help you capitalize on errors—it's like when you get hot playing ping-pong and can't miss no matter what else happens. For some reason even extremely bad shots work for you.

In another instance, Sidney Jones of Pittsburgh always wanted to be a successful salesman. Although he worked on the sales staff of a large manufacturing company, he really wasn't very successful and had absolutely no confidence. His home life was also suffering. His wife had left him because he just wasn't bringing in enough money, bill collectors were constantly hounding him for debts he had run up several years earlier, and his landlord threatened to kick him out if he didn't keep the rent current.

Sidney, however, wanted to make good in the worst way. "I was lying in bed one night," Sidney said, "thinking about the mess I had gotten myself into and wondering just what I could do to increase my sales and my income. Then it hit me—if I could have a series of successes, I would build up so much momentum I couldn't lose.

Next morning I sat down and made out a list of clients I knew I could sell, then went out and sold them. By the end of the day, I was going so strong that even though the next two sales were a lot harder, I simply whizzed right through." Using this system, Sidney's sales suddenly skyrocketed. At the end of the first month he was the number 5 salesman in the company, by the end of three months number 2, and by the end of the first year he had broken all records and was on his way to really big money.

"The important point, I believe," Sidney explained, "is to tackle the easiest prospects first so you build a string of successes and go on to the harder ones with the feeling that you can't lose."

The secret of getting that winning feeling, then, is to build up success patterns and keep them going.

People who want to do something tremendous know they must start gradually and increase as they go along. Weight lifters start with weights they can lift, and gradually increase these over a period of time.

We can apply the same principles—pick a task in the beginning that you can succeed at, then go on from there to more difficult things; tackle pushovers first. Later you can take on that big deal in which you have only a 50-50 chance. The important thing is to get that "winning feeling" *ingrained into your brain.*

Build Your "Guts" Quotient

There's one other thing you need to be a real success—that's guts. Nothing else! How often have you heard somebody say of a go-getter, "he's really got 'guts'!"

There are several things that make up this guts quotient, and it has to do with continuing to fight no matter what. Here are some of the factors that go into it:

> (1) Don't apologize for what you are—there's nothing to apologize for, so don't. Deal in a positive way; never degrade yourself. If you say, "well, I'm not really very good at this," that's negative—don't do it.

For example, Jim Jacobson, a low-paid high school English teacher from Seattle, Washington, decided to boost his income by starting a part-time clinic in *Better Written Communication* for local businesses. Before long, his income was beginning to approach $40,000 and he had almost more clients than he could handle.

At about this point his brother Bob, a high school journalism teacher, joined him in starting a similar school in a nearby city.

Business spurted at first as it had done for Jim, then suddenly dropped off. On inquiry Jim discovered that none of the clients had any confidence in Bob. He apologized at every session for not being a better teacher and constantly played down what he knew about the subject. Because of this his clients decided quickly that he really must not be any good, and his income dried up to a mere trickle. At the same time, Jim's soared to even greater heights and by the time they broke up their partnership he was well on his way to $60,000 year.

(2) Don't ask somebody if it's all right. If you're dubious about whether you should do it or not, do it anyway. Take the initiative and simply go.

In one instance, two men vying for a promotion in a large company ran into an emergency situation, with a decision needed and the boss away. One wasn't sure because the necessary action required keeping the men overtime. The other simply seized the initiative, got the men out there and did the job. His 'guts,' it turned out, saved the company a very good customer and won himself an immediate $5000 bonus, a $6000 a year raise and a step up on the executive level which eventually resulted in a $34,000 a year annual salary. The other man remained at the $9500 a year level for the next year; then, disappointed at the lack of promotion, quit the company.

(3) Stand on your own feet.

Actually, the man with guts is a very decisive man and his decisions are clear cut. When he talks, you can feel great strength and confidence. Today, it's very popular to try to go both ways at once. But if you intend to make the guts quotient work for you, *you* must stand up for what you believe in—no matter what anyone else says. You must also learn to make decisions that leave no doubt as to what you mean. A good example of this is Jack Benton, an aircraft company employee, who opened a part-time advertising agency and landed his first client, a small company who wanted to market a chewable dentifrice. Jack agreed to take the account, but insisted they launch the campaign just before Christmas. The company executives said they simply wouldn't back him in this. After making a thorough study, however, Jack stood his ground, and launched the campaign in October by saturating business magazines with news releases and stories about the product. The result was hundreds of orders, and a furor that few other products ever created. The reason: business magazines are aimed at retailers who buy for Christmas long before the season. Since the December issues contain less advertising than most others, Jack's releases received a far wider audience than they normally would have. If Jack hadn't stood up to the company executives, however, his results would have been extremely mediocre. As it turned out, he not only launched his new agency with a good account but, because of this initial success, also soon attracted two additional million dollar accounts which pushed his personal income over the next six months over the $50,000 level—a far cry from his old $8000 a year job on the aircraft assembly line.

(4) Use your nerve! We've heard people say if they'd known how much trouble they were going to have with some chore, they would never have tried it.

There's a truism here. Sometimes it's better to simply go ahead and do it without knowing too much about the situation.

For instance, suppose you learn that by taking one action you're going to step on one man's toes, and by taking another you'll step on someone else's. Knowing this, you may not do anything.

If you'd come in without knowing this, however, you would have simply gone ahead and acted. And that's what you've got to do—act as if you don't know the problems.

Jake Hamilton, a Portland, Oregon bookkeeper, for instance, picked up extra cash on weekends by selling pictures of local stores' merchandise displays to national business magazines. Over the years Jake had learned that Safeway and Payless Drug Store wouldn't permit pictures. One day, however, he discovered several dozen pictures from these same stores in "his" magazines. On inquiry, he discovered the photographer, Sidney Harold, a friend of his, hadn't been held back by the knowledge that he couldn't take pictures. He simply assumed he could, walked in, shot them, and immediately came out with several thousand dollars.

In many cases you can ride through, with no mishaps, by just doing. *Ignore;* ignore what others think, ignore the consequences of the step you're taking, ignore weaknesses in the plan, and simply go.

(5) Stick to your guns. You hardly ever succeed on the first try. Usually you have to do it over and over again. Look back on your successes. Didn't nearly every one follow a series of failures? By repeating the procedure and correcting the faults each time, you finally made it work. Perseverence can be blind, and probably should be. If you think you're on the right track, ignore the problems and simply go.

Bill Jenkins, an $8000 a year California factory worker deeply in debt, saddled with a broken down old car and faced with the prospect of a long layoff, became convinced he could make money selling recreational land. He then formed his own company and started selling part-time in the evenings for several firms. Despite his enthusiasm, however, Bill made only $3,000 a year for the first three years. But Bill wouldn't give up. The fourth year he hit on the idea of putting on investment seminars at local hotels. He advertised in the newspaper and at the seminars stressed investing for the future instead of buying land. The results: Bill made $40,000 part-time that year, $80,000 the next.

Today Bill lives in an $80,000 home, drives a fancy car and makes a five figure income that is far beyond anything he'd ever dreamed of back in the low-paid factory days.

Be Selfish

The only way you're really going to get ahead is to view every situation as if it belongs to you. Face to face with a strange problem, a scary task, or an uncertain development, just say to yourself: "This is my job, my man, my answer, my territory—the whole thing belongs to me!"—then step in and take it. You'll be surprised how often this technique works.

Stop Being Afraid

This may sound silly, but it isn't. Everybody is afraid. The other man is afraid that you'll notice his tie isn't straight, that his shirt isn't quite pressed, that his shoes aren't quite shined—in other words, everybody is a little bit timid.

But think back. Haven't there been times when you felt that you're the only one who has fears? In actuality, everyone is just as afraid as you are. And not only that, he isn't thinking about you, he's thinking about himself. Since your fears are based on caring, and, really, nobody cares—then you have no fears.

So rout timidity—the only thing to be afraid of is fear itself. Fear gives you an awkwardness, a lack of direction, and a loss of control.

When you're afraid you can't do your best, and your guts quotient can't come forward as it should. The secret here is to force yourself to do a thing by committing yourself to a course of action from which you can't withdraw.

Ken Cook, President of Rent-it Service, San Diego, Calif., used this device quite effectively a few years ago, by letting a magazine come out with a story stating that in four years he would be doing ten million dollars' worth of business per year. Once Cook had committed himself this way, he had to live up to the goal or face humiliation in front of the entire industry.

Practice Pushing Yourself
Whenever Possible

Pushing yourself is a habit. The man who's going someplace always seems to be at the right place at the right time, making the right deals. This is because he's gotten into the habit of pushing himself forward. You must do this, too—start now. Whenever there's something to do, volunteer—serve on that committee, put out that brochure, make that speech. In other words, push yourself forward at all times and go that one step farther.

Checking On Chapter 3

1. Set yourself a goal—decide what you want to do, and your subconscious will help you get there.
2. Build your self-image—do this by spending 30 minutes every day seeing yourself as you want to be—pay close attention to small details.
3. Utilize the power of conscious thinking—you can make your conscious thoughts work for you by going over and over until they become an intense, burning desire.
4. Start building your success personality:

    A. Develop a feeling of nostalgia for the future.
    B. See yourself as a successful person.
    C. Remember the success—forget the failures.
    D. Don't let your mistakes become you.

5. Use enthusiasm as a money-making tool. Here are the rules:

   A. Get excited—don't wonder in advance what you're going to say, just open your mouth and say it.
   B. Speak louder than usual.
   C. Try banging something.
   D. Be a child again.

6. Get that winning feeling. Do it by putting a whole string of successes together before you tackle the harder tasks. Once you get into the habit of winning, you'll find it hard to lose.

7. Build your "guts" quotient this way:

   A. Don't apologize for what you are.
   B. Don't ask—do it.
   C. Stand on your own feet.
   D. Use your nerve—act without knowing.
   E. Stick to your guns.

8. Be selfish—the best way to get ahead is to believe you deserve it.

9. Stop being afraid— everybody is afraid, and few pay any attention to you.

10. Push yourself forward—get into the habit of stepping forward at every point.

Chapter 4

How to Come Up With
Big Money-Making Ideas

Is it possible to get rich working for somebody else? You bet it is! There are people who make $180,000 to $500,000 a year or more, as presidents of some companies; vice-presidents often make good money. But just remember, working for somebody else is the difficult way to do it. After all, there are only about 500 top executive jobs in the United States today making $100,000 a year or more.

If that's true, then, where can you make good money?

Well, there are other places! One is commission sales. Here you have the potential to make unlimited amounts.

Alex Houston, for example, turned down a regular salary, because as he said, he "could only make peanuts that way." He took over a territory selling Materials Handling Equipment, part-time for a well-known company, and made $20,000 the first year, $40,000 the second, and $100,000 the year after—all by tapping market areas that had never been tried before. This only works when you're on commission and the company agrees not to limit you.

Despite the possibility in sales, however, the best place to make good by working part-time is in your own business.

Bob Ronson, for instance, working as a plumber for an Aero-Space industry at $10,000 a year and in desperate need of more money to finance his daughter's college education, took over a small gas station in addition to his regular job. He invested $500 cash, and just three hours a day to supervise employees, put in a number of used cars brought to him on consignment by their owners, and within eight years turned the whole thing into an eight million dollar investment with 25 lots.

James Bunion, a teacher making $8,200 a year who needed an extra $16,000 to pay for a delicate heart operation for his infant son, started a delivery service in the late afternoons (three hours a day) for businessmen who needed extra-special handling for their merchandise—within four months, James took in a partner, bought two trucks and soon zoomed the business to the million dollar mark.

You, of course, can do the same—but in the beginning think of your spare-time fortune in terms of what you can actually do.

Check These Money-Making Areas

Just where can you look when you're searching for spare-time fortune ideas? The answer is practically everywhere. The trick is to pick out something you really like to do, and which fits your individual talents.

Now, consider these general money-making areas. Then we'll give you some guidelines to use in deciding which ones are for you.

Mail Order

This is an attractive spare-time business possibility. You can start with practically nothing (as little as $50) and sell such things as lures, novelty items, books, toys and other products by placing classified ads in such magazines as *Popular Science,* and larger ads in the mail order sections of magazines like *Better Homes and Gardens*

Utilizing the facilities available in your garage or kitchen and working on your own a few hours a week, evenings or Saturdays, you can put together a mail order business that will earn you $5000, $10,000 or $20,000 a year. In the past, many first timers starting from scratch with practically no money have propelled themselves to mail order fortunes. And some, like E. Joseph Cossman, have made as much as a million dollars or more.

A quick glance at magazine mail order columns of just three magazines, *American Home, Family Circle* and *Popular Mechanics,* shows the following: rugs, do-it-yourself kits, zodiac samplers, a watch calendar, a baby's hobby horse, mice pin cushions and more.

Getting into the mail order business is fairly simple—find a product, test it, develop the product, sell and promote it.

To detail this a bit more, start your own mail order business by looking at the mail order ads in such magazines as *Better Homes & Gardens, The Los Angeles Times Home Section* and others. Try to remember the needs of the consumers who make up America. Then start looking for a product. You can find these by attending trade shows and seeing what's being promoted there. Also, look at your own locality as a possible idea source. For instance, one Hollywood firm cashes in on the city's reputation by selling movie posters, a mail order house in New England built a fantastic business selling live lobsters through the mail, and a New Mexico company sells Indian wares.

Next, check back issues of magazines (up to ten years old) like *Popular Science* and *Popular Mechanics*—many products advertised there can be promoted again.

Finally, you'll find colleges and universities excellent sources, since many universities consistantly come up with new research ideas that can be developed into salable products.

Test your product by making up a few samples and placing them in local stores on consignment (simply go in and ask the owner or manager), rent a booth at a local fair ($25 to $100), offer your product to mail order houses, rent space at a local "outdoor market" ($2 to $10), make up a sample and run ads locally (from $2 to several hundred dollars), or make up a new product news release (about $35, see complete details on this in Chapter 9), and send off a few to magazines whose readers might be interested. From these responses you can get an idea about how well your product will do.

Once you decide to go ahead, develop your product by letting others do as much work as possible. First, go to the library and look up all the possible business magazines covering your product in *Ayers Standard Rate and Data Service. Toys and Novelties Magazine, Playthings* and several others cover the toy field, *Lawn/Garden/Outdoor Living, Home and Garden Merchandiser,* plus others in the lawn and garden field, *Sports Age, Selling Sporting Goods, Sporting Goods Business* and a number of others in the sports field. These magazines can give you the names and addresses of suppliers in the field. Many of these suppliers are experts and can save you years of development time. If you're going to produce the item yourself, get as many bids as you can. If possible, don't do any manufacturing, but farm out all phases. If you're developing a Whip Top toy, for instance, you can farm the top and the whip out to one company, the packaging to another. Often your suppliers can tell you whom to go to for these services (for complete details, see Chapters 6 and 7 on developing and testing your ideas).

Services You Can Start With Only Your Own Labor

These are excellent because they can be started with almost no capital. Baby-sitting services, lawn and garden services, a secretarial service, answering services, janitorial services, nearly new shop-at-home services and more. You can get into all of these with a minimum of equipment and mostly your own labor.

What can you make? That depends upon your own ability and imagination: One low-paid factory worker with a pile of debts and a limited salary decided to utilize a vacant lot he'd purchased with $100 down for trailer parking. By the end of the first year he was "trailer sitting" twenty trailers at $15 a month and had already pocketed $2000 that year.

A janitor for a local school district who needed extra cash above and beyond his meager salary to pay for car repairs, started a handbill distribution service for local merchants with $35. Within four months he was grossing $800 a month.

A young fifth grade teacher with a wife who needed special nursing care decided to supplement his less than $7000 a year paycheck by putting out a small newspaper for several local merchants. Beginning with $15, he soon was clearing over $600 extra a month. The book *100 Ways to Make Money in Your Spare Time Starting With Less Than $100* by Stockwell and Holtje (Parker Publishing Co.) will help you find part-time services you can start on a shoestring.

In considering any of these, make sure you're qualified. In starting a secretarial service, for instance, you should know how to take dictation, type, perform mimeographing, multilithing and all types of duplicating services. You can start this service with a typewriter, desk, chair, table and other equipment on an original investment of just a few dollars. Begin by sending out letters announcing your services. Also post notices in office buildings, lobbies, schools, colleges and convention halls. Other businesses of this type can be started and promoted the same way.

Promoting Your Hobby

Here's a field that offers good opportunities for an investment of practically pocket change. If you're a skin or scuba diver, like to surf, have a photographic hobby, collect coins, stamps, build models or like pets, you can turn these hobbies into part-time businesses: $25-$50 an hour taking wedding photos, $5-$10 an hour dog walking, $15-$25 an hour pet grooming, $30-$50 an hour conducting Kiddy puppet and magic shows, $5-$10 an hour taking news pictures for local newspapers. Start by looking carefully at your present hobbies and decide which you would like to pursue as a business. Next, decide which part of your hobby is marketable.

One surfing enthusiast, an $8000 a year box company worker, simply got tired of spending all his time on a low-paid, unrewarding factory job, and decided to do something better with his life. He started by making up a large sign that said: *"Are you a surfing beginner? Expert Lessons—$4.00."* He then took this to a beach and organized one hour classes of ten people each. Later he moved to a private beach and set up a rather elaborate surfing school arrangement—last I heard of him, he had five instructors and was averaging $600 a weekend!

Another enthusiast tired of eking out a meager living driving a bus, took his $100 savings, found the biggest beach he could, made a down payment on twelve used surfboards, re-painted them and started a surfboard rental service. After the first few months he paid for his boards and plowed everything back. Now he owns an impressive-looking surfboard rental shop in a popular beach area that grosses well over $100,000 a year. College kids run it for him, so he can devote his time to developing other businesses.

Other possibilities here: sales, service and surfboard repairing. In building up any hobby business, start slowly in a practical, easy way.

After you decide on something, figure out if there's a demand and how you can reach the market. With the surfboard lessons, all that was needed was a big sign. Each approach is different, but it must always be easy and simple, and you must be able to reach a good-sized market at small cost.

Direct Sales

Here's an overlooked field. Since many companies will start you with free samples, direct sales can be started with practically no cash. They also can be handled successfully in as little as an hour a day. Possibilities include: selling signs to businesses ($50 to $150 a week), cleaning equipment ($30 to $200 a week), rubber stamps ($50 to $200 a week), advertising gimmicks to business (imprinted pens, rulers, etc. $20 to $150 a week), matchbook advertising ($50 to $500 a week), jewelry ($10 to $150 a week), kitchenware ($10 to $170 a week), cosmetics ($25 to $300 a week).

Tom Bolton, a $5000 a year deliveryman who got tired of never being able to afford decent clothes for his children and of living in a run-down house in a slum neighborhood, decided to start selling greetings cards door-to-door in his spare time. He then expanded the line to include other kinds of cards. After that he added stationery, monogrammed labels, rubber stamps and other items. To display these, he made up a well-organized presentation kit and hired two salesmen. That first year Tom earned $15,000 above all expenses, the next year $25,000. By the end of the fourth year Tom had almost $70,000 in the bank, a luxurious home in a swanky neighborhood and an income that far exceeded his wildest dreams.

The steps:

a. Pick a product (*Specialty Salesman's Magazine* and *Salesman's Opportunity* offer dozens).

b. Decide how you can work up a complete line. This means adding many related items in the same category until you have enough to reasonably expect a good income. For instance, say you start out selling advertising book matches to businesses. You may also add other merchandise featuring this same kind of advertising, such as calendars, name plates, pens and pencils, ash trays and rulers, plus post card advertising, car and window signs, and more. The rule simply is, add all the related items you can think of and can handle easily.

c. Build sales. You will have to "road test" it yourself. That is, you will have to establish regular routes, make the initial contacts and, in general, build up your business until it's doing well enough to hire other salesmen.

d. Hire your own sales force. When you have worked out the kinks as to what products you should sell, the best way to make sales, who to see, how to deliver, plus all other details, and are really making it pay, you can then consider hiring a salesman. At this point you will have the know-how to show others how to do it.

Tutoring

This may seem like a strange part-time business opportunity, but think it over. In today's highly technical world, many people need help learning a specialized field. Maybe you're good at math (parents are often willing to hire a tutor for their kids). Or perhaps you know a language or are good at music or art—all of these are salable commodities.

Ben Thompson, for instance, an Ohio bank teller earning $125 a week, had played the trumpet as a hobby ever since high school, but had never thought of it in terms of money-making possibilities. Then one day he discovered his son needed an immediate $10,000 operation. He was already over $1000 in debt, with little possibility of borrowing much more. It was at this point that he decided to take a chance. As a result he inserted an ad in the local paper advertising trumpet lessons, and soon had more students than he could handle. Shortly afterward he hired another musician part-time, and later expanded into a five instructor school, bringing him an automatic income (automatic because others make the money for him) of $30,000 a year.

You can start a tutoring business by simply deciding what you know well that's in demand—are you a wizard in math? Is English your specialty? Are you good at dancing? What? Advertise by using a classified ad in the local newspaper for about $1, or put a notice on the bulletin board at the local schools, colleges and churches.

Helping People Get Together

There's no greater need today than helping other people meet each other. Tremendous "Get Together" businesses have grown out of this, including computerized dating services, night clubs and resorts catering to singles. You can't start a resort in the beginning, of course, but there are things you can do that will bring in immediate money.

For instance, did you ever think of a service for young girls and single servicemen overseas who want to correspond?

Mary Beale, an $80 a week Ohio telephone company employee with two small daughters to raise, did. She contacted the local Red Cross and arranged for them to deliver the first batch of letters. She then dug up correspondents by placing small classified ads in the paper and by inserting cards on bulletin boards of the telephone company and others, asking for young girls who would like to correspond with servicemen overseas. She charged five dollars for the initial contact and one dollar each for all others. This fee also entitled them to a year's membership in the "Overseas Friendship Club," which held regular meetings to exchange information and names with other girls like themselves. Today Mary is in the $25,000 a year bracket.

Another possibility is a computer dating service. One enterprising young man, Lee Douglass, a low-paid key punch operator with a drawer full of bills and no future, started by simply renting computer space from a local computer center. He programmed the computer initially by asking 200 residents of a local "singles" apartment to fill out the forms, in return for two months free use of the service. After that he advertised his service with ads in the local paper, saying: "Meet a member of the opposite sex you'll really like." Information from new enrollees, of course, was then fed into the computer to build up the "dating bank" at $250 per new member. Lee Douglass today has over 50,000 clients and is currently earning over $100,000 a year.

There are many variations to this, such as computerizing personal information among several single groups for a fee, and matching partners for perfect dates at group affairs, offering several campuses at once computerized dating through ads in the local college papers, setting up computerized dating for the "Formerly Marrieds," and more.

The steps: Decide on a definite need, set up the mechanics of the service, then figure out how to reach your audience.

Help People Swap Things

You'll find many variations. It consists simply of providing a way for people to turn in what they don't want for what they do. This can take the form of a classified newspaper, published for as little as $35 an issue, where people list what they have and what they want.

In a variation of this, Mr. and Mrs. Glen Russell advertised for old things on consignment (in the local paper). They then took them to a local flea market, marked them up 30 percent and sold them. They kept the 30 percent and turned the rest back to the people providing the merchandise. Before hitting on this idea,

Glen was struggling along on a $6800 a year salary as a school janitor, trying to pay off some astronomical hospital bills. Today, Glen makes more than this amount from his part-time business. He paid off the hospital debts the first year, now buys a brand new car every year, and is putting two daughters through college.

Another couple, Irwin and Sue Miller, clipped want ads, pasted these on a sheet and passed them out in local supermarkets. This was the beginning of a paper called *The Trading Post,* which grew to seven pages a week. By the end of the first year this newspaper had supplemented Irv's salary as a fork lift operator at a local warehouse by almost $4000 and allowed him to finance a trip from Europe for his mother, whom he hadn't seen in twenty years. Today Irwin and Sue live in a $65,000 home and take trips to Europe themselves almost every year.

Bill Wilton, for instance, who saw no future in his low-paying job with the post office, prepared a sample company newsletter and contacted all the companies and organizations in his area by mail. The result—fifteen called him at home for a further look-see. Using his annual leave, he took two days off to see each of the companies and sold five monthly newsletters at $200 each. By the end of the year his part-time income passed $10,000. Since he was already getting an army retirement check, Bill quit the post office job and began to put full time into promoting his newsletter. This effort netted $25,000 the next year. Bill soon paid off debts that had been plaguing him for many years and now finds himself on easy street.

The companies that Bill puts out the newsletters for have the responsibility of furnishing the news. They do this by appointing an employee in each department as a reporter. Bill then sifts through what comes in and selects the best. There are many variations to this, including helping retail stores communicate with their customers and more.

Recreation

This is also a field that commands big money—it includes camper and trailer manufacturers, private campgrounds, bowling alleys and more. For spare-time recreational opportunities, you can start with little capital. Consider recreation rentals.

One couple, Mr. and Mrs. Kay Bohrer, noticed while visiting their favorite mountain resort that all the kids had nowhere to play but in the lodge parking lot and really needed some type of organized activity. They drove 100 miles to the nearest big town, bought 50 skateboards for $39 and set up a skateboard rental. The result: a complete sellout at an unused end of the lot, and a brand new business they conducted under a lease arrangement with the lodge. Every summer they add an extra $400 to their income by making the vacation pay for itself.

People looking for spare time incomes have rented bicycles, canoes, motorbikes, minibikes, archery equipment, badminton sets and more. The trick is to find a recreational area with a clear need—get permission from the resort (you usually have to pay a fee of $10 up), set it up, and see how it goes.

Repair Services

What a field this is! There's a tremendous need here for the repair of such items as toasters, electric coffee pots, tape recorders, washing machines, driers and similar items.

We've gotten to the point in America today where we're going to need more and more repairmen just to keep up with demand. It is possible to make money if you can do a lot of repairing in a short time. This could mean working out standard repairs for popular makes that can be used again and again, or limiting repairs to only certain appliances for which you have worked out advance fast repair methods. Courses available in most adult education departments can give you the technical know-how.

Clean-Up Services

You'll also find a big demand here. The public needs attic, yard and basement clean-up, small apartment and office building services and others. Often you can begin with an investment of as low as $300 for used equipment and an old station wagon or pickup.

A subscription or copy of Building Services Contractor Magazine, 101 West 31st St., New York, N.Y. 10001, will help introduce you to the field and give you the addresses of janitorial and equipment suppliers. To price properly, decide what kind of work you intend to do: homes, offices, doctors' offices, supermarkets, windows, etc. Then call several small cleaning services (located through the yellow pages), and ask their prices for various kinds of jobs. Discount these prices about 25 percent. This will be your starting figure.

Once you have experience, decide how long it takes you to do particular jobs, how much janitorial supplies cost, equipment payments and depreciation, and come up with your own rates. To be extremely competitive, always try to stay 5 percent to 10 percent below competition.

You will find several problems—unsteady and untrained help, the tendency of clients to price chisel, and your own temptation to bid too low on competitive jobs. You can solve the personnel problem by requiring all potential employees to fill out an employment application (obtained at any office supply store), and hire only those who show signs of permanence. Solve the pricing problem by establishing a fair fee that yields reasonable profit.

The best way to start is to decide what equipment you need, place an ad in the yellow pages, print up a small brochure and take it around to your potential customers. The rest pretty well takes care of itself.

Budget Help

With the advent of the bank card and extensive credit, you'll find many people in deep financial trouble today. If you're good at this, you might try offering some budget help. The best way to make contact is an ad, under "Personal," in the local paper. This can grow into a financial counselor's service or related business.

Writing and Editing Services

Freelance magazine writing is difficult and doesn't offer immediate money, but local "cash and carry" writing does. Students, for instance, often need help in the editing and re-typing of reports, themes, theses, and similar material. Local people need speeches written and job seekers need resumes. All pay when your client picks up his material. If you lean in this direction, simply put your name in the yellow pages, under "writer," and see what happens. To do this, have your residental phone changed to a business listing. This will cost a few dollars more a month, but includes an automatic listing in the yellow pages.

How To Come Up With Money-Making Ideas

Here are some ways to find ideas:

Check newspaper ads thoroughly. By looking through newspaper want ads, you will find many ideas relating to the thirteen areas above which you can turn into money-making possibilities.

In looking through a recent issue of my local paper, I found an ad which said: *"Let George Do It—Light Hauling and Garage Cleaning."* If this man can make money hauling, so can you. Get yourself a pickup truck, put an ad in the paper and go to work.

Another says: *"Auction Saturday—all sorts of household items."* You can certainly hold one of these yourself from items you've accumulated, or build a business by running your own ad for items to auction off.

Utilize the public library. You'll find your public library an important place to find ideas. Don't, however, try to find an idea through time-consuming research. Simply go through and let anything you run into suggest a possible money-making category.

On a recent browsing trip, for instance, we picked up "How To Get $50,000 Worth of Services Each Year From The U.S. Government," and found a pamphlet listing future jobs for high school girls—let your imagination play with this one. Will girls need pamphlets on different kinds of jobs? Will they need a counseling service? How about a resume service to help them get started?

Next, we found a book on pleasure boating in Tennessee. Let this trigger you. Think of all the boats on water and their needs. Maybe a small "coffee boat" would make a good weekend business, or a bait boat. When using the library to find part-time possibilities, you must use your imagination and start asking yourself questions in all directions.

In addition, of course, libraries have collections of pamphlets and magazines. Tell your librarian what you want, and browse.

Attend trade fairs and shows. This is a great place to come up with ideas. Distributors often show their latest wares and frequently turn up ideas you can use. Depending on the show, you'll find people pushing ant farms, shrunken heads, tractors, scented soap and more.

At one stationery manufacturer's trade show, for instance, E. Joseph Cossman, a prominent mail order executive looking for ideas, noticed that many of the items shown carried a circus theme. Since the movie "The Greatest Show On Earth" was about to be released, he decided to take advantage of all the circus publicity and jumped on the bandwagon with a set of plastic circus figurines. This item promptly became his top mail order seller for that year.

Although circus toys had no relationship with the stationery field, he got the idea by visiting a trade show. At trade shows you can come up with ideas for products, services and many other things.

Go through the telephone yellow pages. In the telephone yellow pages you can see what other people are doing. Let their activities suggest part-time business possibilities.

Here are a few from the San Francisco directory:

a. Bridal gown preservation service (you might start one of these in cities where none is available).
b. Buz's charter rental (how about putting together some fun tours, chartering a bus and seeing what happens).
c. Carnival supplies—big savings for P.T.A., schools, churches and clubs (this could make a good part-time business just as it is; also, flower rentals, table decoration services, and more).

Any telephone directory will yield dozens like these which you can turn into money.

Read magazines regularly. Popular Mechanics, Mechanix Illustrated and *Popular Science* magazines offer many ideas. Both advertisements and articles suggest good part-time money-making activities.

Here are a few possibilities from past issues:

Be a recreational director, sports, crafts, camp nature leader. An ad that might suggest setting up your own summer recreation program for neighborhood kids at a fee ($25 each), starting a course for people who want to be recreational directors ($100 to $300), or taking kids on weekend trips ($25 each)—possibilities are river canoe trips, guided nature tours, and more. This type of activity allows you to make an extra $2000 or $3000 in your spare time for summer fun, and yet have practically the whole year left to enjoy it.

Art from old furniture. An article. People here are using doorknobs, porch posts, door pulls, and much else to create unusual art (it might suggest making and selling these items yourself, or starting classes for housewives.) $1000 to $7000 extra a year.

Build, refinish, restore anything of wood. An ad. Start a community refinishing service, or set up classes for housewives who want to refinish their own furniture. Furniture finishers who know their business can charge $8 to $25 an hour, and several who also combine finishing with classes have run their take from this business into a tidy fortune of $20,000 a year and more.

What kind of ATV is best for you? An article. Set up an ATV–all terrain vehicle–rental in a vacation area, put on a trade show (at a fee) for ATV dealers in your area, or put on guided ATV trips into back country mountain areas. You can also sell ATVs (costing $700 up) or expand into all types of recreational vehicles: trailers ($1000 to $8000), truck campers ($700 up), motor homes ($3500 to $15,000). The beauty of selling this kind of item, of course, is that you don't have to sell very many to make a bundle.

Defender of Women—assailants run screaming when sprayed in the face with Defender. An ad (sell defense items for women by mail–set up self-defense classes for women in a local gym). You can charge so much per class, say $10 or $15, or a flat fee of from $200 to $500 for a series of classes. A class of ten for ten weeks at a flat fee of $200 would net you a cool $2000, and this is just the beginning.

You'll find dozens of these tips in every issue, each of which will yield several possible money-making ideas. Simply take the original idea and turn it in several directions to see if you can come up with something which will work for you.

Check magazine "new products" sections. This is almost the same thing as reading the magazines themselves, but not quite. Companies and individuals offering new products and new ideas often place them here. You'll find these under the heading of "What's New," "What's Different," or something similar.

Read trade magazines. In addition to the popular magazines, consider trade (business) magazines. Items here are aimed primarily at retailers, manufacturers or wholesalers. They are intended to help these people in their business, but turned right, they may prove to be a gold mine for you.

Look for the deficiencies around you. Take a look at your city and neighborhood. What do they need that isn't provided? Look at the streets and the curbs—are the curb numbers in good shape or are they getting old? This ought to suggest the possibility of making up number stencils, hiring a few boys, and painting the curbs for $1.00 each. Multiply this by the number of houses in a typical housing development and you'll get a vague idea of the money-making possibilities of this kind of service in a typical community.

Here's another: How many rental bicycles do you find in your city? If you don't find any, why not lease a small piece of a service station, arrange to lease some used bikes from a local bike shop and give it a try. In some cities, this one idea alone can be worth $1000 to $10,000 to any enterprising part-time businessman who wants to cash in.

In any area, of course, you can come up with dozens of additional items.

Keep needs in mind. In a neighborhood where mothers can't get out because of the kids, they can always use a daytime baby-sitting service. The demand is tremendous and you needn't do the sitting yourself. As a baby sitting coordinator you simply arrange "sittings" for women and girls and take a percentage of their earnings, which can amount to an extra $1000-$6000 a year and more.

In mountain campgrounds during the summer, the need and desire of campers to keep up with what's going on in the world always creates a demand for a campground newspaper delivery service ($20 to $500 extra a month). And the natural tendency of some people not to pay their bills creates a need among small merchants for someone (besides a regular collection service) to help them collect ($50 to $1000 a month).

You can add dozens more.

Make a list of things you'd like to do, as you find them. Keep a notebook handy at all times, and as you discover money-making possibilities, jot them down.

A few random thoughts from my own notebook are:

> Buy a run-down hotel in a small town (not too far from a metropolitan city), hire a recreational director and get guests really involved with games, singing and similar activities.
> Start a private campground.
> Start a canoe rental service at a nearby recreation lake.
> Sell do-it-yourself plans of all sorts.
> Consider the money-making possibilities of a small bus (busing people to particular places, picking up things, etc.).

Now, start your own notebook and see what you can come up with.

Use "brain busting" to come up with an idea list. This is simple. Get yourself a blackboard—start writing down any money-making idea that pops into your mind, no matter how wild. Your list might look something like this:

    a. Sell wild birds.
    b. Set up a bicycle tire fix-it service for neighborhood kids.
    c. Paint telephone poles black.
    d. Run cars in for lube jobs.
    e. Put a toll gate in front of your house.
    f. Print up a specialized map of your city.

Some of these are pretty silly, but that's all right. When you get through, just cross those out and keep the good ones, then take a look at some of the variations and see what you can come up with in the way of practical ideas.

Make Sure Each Final Idea
Is Something You Can Do

Spare-time job ideas are great, but they won't do you any good unless you can actually put them in operation.

Let's say you listed writing a magazine or newspaper column. If you've done quite a few of these and know how to go about them, fine. But if you've never done any writing before, it's not very practical. Cross this off and go on to something you can actually do right now. If you still want to do it, decide what kind of training you'll need and start to prepare.

Now Add A Flare To Each Idea

It's not good enough just to come up with an idea. A common idea, for the most part, will produce common results. If you want it to have zip and attract attention, give it a unique twist.

How can you do this? Many ways—suppose, for instance, you decide to rent inflatable life rafts during the vacation season. Since most rafts are yellow, you can make yours different by painting them red. Another twist—put in a sliding window, facing your parking lot. Paint some lines and advertise it as a drive-in raft rental service.

Make Sure Each Idea Is
Really Money-Oriented

It's not enough just to come up with a workable idea. Anything you do should also have good money-making possibilities. Ask yourself these questions before you go any further:

1. Can I handle the idea easily without extra training or equipment?
2. Can I charge enough to bring in a profit?
3. Will people put themselves out to buy these services?
4. Is the price right?
5. Does it offer something extra?

Is there really good money in this—check it over again and ask yourself honestly if it really has a chance. If it doesn't, go into something else.

Checking On Chapter 4

1. You can make a spare-time fortune either through commission sales or your own enterprise.
2. These thirteen general money-making areas offer possibilities:

    a. Mail order.
    b. Services.
    c. Hobbies.
    d. Direct sales.
    e. Tutoring.
    f. Get-together services.
    g. Swapping and auction services.
    h. Communications.
    i. Recreation.
    j. Repair services.
    k. Clean-up.
    l. Budget help.
    m. Writing and editing.

3. Now, here are the ways to come up with money-making ideas:

    a. Check newspaper want ads thoroughly.
    b. Utilize the public library.
    c. Attend trade shows and fairs.
    d. Go through the Telephone Yellow Pages.
    e. Read magazines regularly.
    f. Check magazine New Product sections.
    g. Read trade magazines.
    h. Keep needs in mind.
    i. Make a list of things as you find them.

j. Use brain busting.

4. Make sure each final idea is practical—you must actually be able to do it.

5. Add a flair to each—to give it added oomph; each idea should have something a little extra. For a drive-in restaurant, for instance, this extra could be as simple as a teenager in a bear suit urging people to come on in—every idea, however, does need a flair.

6. Make sure each idea is money-oriented—try to make sure it will actually make money.

Chapter 5

How to Choose Your Wealth Goals--
Today!

Today there are thousands of part-time projects around that can be turned into big money. The problem, of course, is that they're not all suitable for you. You'll find some too difficult, some require too much capital, others demand too specialized a knowledge, and still others just aren't anything you'd really enjoy.

What you must do, of course, is weed out those projects that already have one strike against them, and pick only those that give you the best possible chance for success.

Check The Idea Against What
You Can Actually Do

First, you must take the ideas you come up with and look them over carefully to see if they are practical projects for you.

Suppose, for instance, you decide that you'd like to grow trees in containers and sell them at a local "farmer's market."

Okay, then write down all the steps you'll have to go through. Your list might look something like this:

1. Find where to purchase stock.
2. Buy trees.
3. Find and buy necessary equipment.
4. Make up soil mix.
5. Pot trees.
6. Water daily.
7. Build some sort of shelter.

8. Miscellaneous care.
9. Get them ready for market.
10. Contact and light up market.
11. Transport.
12. Set up and sell.

Now run down this list and see if there's any activity here you'd have trouble doing. Suppose, for instance, you're in the habit of going away every weekend. Naturally, then, you're going to have trouble watering every day.

You can, of course, hire a neighborhood boy to water for you. You can give up your weekend trips. Or you can decide that none of these is practical and you should look for some other project.

As another example, if you decide you would like to lecture for money, you'll find there are many places where you can break down. You may not be enough of an expert, you may be unable to convince one of the agencies to take you on—you may want to talk about something that may not be of much interest, and more.

In other words, you're stopped before you start if you can't measure up at every step.

Make Sure It's Practical

Many projects look great until you realize they're entirely impractical. Suppose, for instance, you want to start a mail order business with a particular product. To get that product you must put up a $5,000 deposit that you don't have. For the moment, then, this project becomes impractical. Forget it until you actually have the cash available.

As another example, you might decide to ship food products by mail, and then find local laws prohibit this in some areas. This might cut possible profit to the point where it would prove impractical.

Now look at every step on your list closely to make sure it really is practical. To show you what we mean, let's go back to the tree project. For instance:

(1) Can you find suppliers? Call up the state forestry right now and ask them who supplies small trees and where you can buy them. If there are suppliers available and you can get to them, that's fine.

(2) Can you get the trees shipped to where you are? Write a letter or call and see.

(3) Next, go to the planting of trees. What kind of containers

are you going to use? Are they available? Are they cheap enough?

If you use milk cartons, for instance, what's your source? Can you get them from a restaurant that throws them away? Will they give them to you?

(4) What about the soil? Call up a local nursery and see what you need, or call the farm adviser in your area and get the soil requirements. Can you get this soil easily? Is it available without cost? Are you going to do it yourself, or have it done? If so, what's the cost?

Simply lay out each step, piece by piece, and ask yourself seven or eight questions under each. Make sure everything is detailed. Also, make sure that everything is all right before you go farther. If you run into a step that can't be solved, quit now. It's better to do it at this stage than to run into the problem once you've got real money and time invested.

Compare Your Idea To Others That Are Making Money

Here's a dandy way to cut the risk. If you'd like to start a baby-sitting service, for instance, find someone who's already in the business by checking the newspaper want ads. Then call and see if you can talk to them in person and ask questions. You should find out: how much it costs to start, where their customers are coming from, how many customers they need to make a profit, if they're really making money, exactly how much work it is, what problems they're running into, and more.

Now consider it from a money standpoint. How much are they making for their time? If it's under $5 an hour, you should consider the business carefully before actually trying.

If it passes the money test, however, then ask yourself: "Can I do it better? Can I give better service? Can I offer it at a better price? Can I do it in a more practical way? Can I add something extra?"

If you can answer yes to these questions, your project will probably have a good chance of success.

Check The Idea Against Your Skill List

To really succeed at something, of course, you must have the skills to handle all the steps. The only way to find out if you do is to go back through your skill list and check each point.

Let's say, for example, you're going to operate a small store with three employees. In general, every small store owner should be able to see the problem areas and be able to initiate new methods. He must have a friendly interest in people and know how to handle and lead employees.

He should be capable of arranging fundamentals in logical order, know how to make up schedules, keep up inventory and establish operating procedures. In addition, he should be willing to work long hours and be able to make quick, accurate decisions. Finally, he must have good physical stamina.

Knowing this much, it's simple to check your skills and see if you have the needed traits. Do this for each project you consider going into.

Decide If It Feels
Right For You

After you've laid out the steps, looked at some of the business possibilities, and taken stock—ask yourself just how you feel about this.

Look over each step individually, then try to determine whether or not you're generally enthusiastic or have some reservations about the project as a whole.

If you don't feel really enthusiastic, I strongly recommend you simply forget it. You're going to need a great deal of energy to get this business started and you want everything possible working for you. Therefore definitely, in the beginning, restrict yourself to those projects you can really get steamed up about. After all, you don't have to take on the first thing you come up with. More important, you want to use that enthusiasm as a tool—after all, enthusiasm and real interest are great motivating factors. Without these two to propel you along, you may well run into trouble later.

How To Analyze The Project
With Your Needs In Mind

To find out if a proposed project will meet your needs, list the things that you want to do, need to do, or like to do.

Do you like to travel? Do you prefer to sit home and handle affairs by phone? Do you like to talk to people, or what? These things should all be considered when you're analyzing projects.

Willard Thompson of Los Angeles was just barely scraping by on his teacher's salary when his daughter came home needing $1000 worth of dental work. At this point Willard felt like the world had fallen in. As a desperation measure he decided to start a part-time mail order business selling children's novelties. The business soared, but began to take more and more time. When it hit $40,000 gross a year he quit his teaching job and began to put in ten hours a day, six days a week.

Willard, however, was still unhappy. His chief interests were travel, fishing, and talking to people—none of which he did much of in his mail order business. After trying to match these two needs for a couple of years, Willard gave up and decided to start selling post card photography to motels and resorts just three days a week.

This suited him well, the business soared, and he cleared $20,000 the first year. In addition he was able to travel and talk to people all the time, and his work schedule gave him plenty of time for the fishing he loved so much.

When considering a project then, first make up a list of what you really enjoy doing, then compare that with the step-by-step list of your projects and make sure you don't find major conflicts.

Use A Good, Better, Best
Big Money Elimination System

By the time you get this far, you should be considering seven or eight possible projects. You've decided which ones you like, compared the ideas against others, and checked them against your skill, feel and need list. Now put them to the final test. Will they really make money? At this stage you will have to guess.

Evaluate your projects as best you can. Then list them under the headings as to how you think they'll do, by *poor, fair, good, better* and *best.*

Suppose, for instance, one of your proposed ideas is to sell jellies and jams from a local stand, another to sell ant farms by mail order.

All right, we will have to guess as to how they'll do, so make an estimate—jams and jelly sales should be steady, but your market will be restricted to the people within easy driving distance of your stand. Realistically, you probably can't ever expect to gross over $15,000 a year, so put this down as only *fair.*

Now you'll find ant farms a different matter. There's still a good market for them among boys and girls. In the past, mail order firms have grossed well over $100,000 on this one item alone. This item can be bought cheaply at quantity discount from a novelty supply house or made for pennies in limited quantities. So the big money possibilities, handled the right way, would probably be very good. I would list it under *better*.

Now suppose you run into a situation where a firm is looking for somebody to handle a sub-contract with a minimum guarantee of $50,000. Since this is immediate, guaranteed, and a definite market, your big money possibilities here are *best*.

Using these examples, go through your own projects and see what you can come up with.

There are lots of wealth-building projects that you can use, but one of your more important steps is to decide which ones are for you, which ones fit your needs and abilities, and whether or not they can actually be done without forcing cost and time out of sight.

Checking On Chapter 5

1. *Make sure you can actually do your selected project*—lay out as many steps as you can think of and see if you can really do them.
2. *Make sure each idea is practical*—you may be able to do it, but it may not be very practical. Consider this carefully.
3. *Compare your idea to others*—check to make sure they're really making money.
4. *Make sure you have the skills to carry out your project.* Doing projects within your skill areas helps give you a head start.
5. *Make sure you really want to do it.* If you're not really enthusiastic, go on to another idea.
6. *Make sure your project takes into account the things you want or like to do.* This includes travel, talking to people, and almost anything else.
7. *Rate your projects*—keep only the best ones.

Chapter 6

How to Guarantee
a Big Money Fortune

Once we decide on an idea that we think is going to make money, we don't rush out and start to work. Now we want to test it to see if the project will do as well as we think it should. If it looks like it will go, we launch into it wholeheartedly—if not, then we test another idea.

After all, how well a project goes depends on many things—the total market for your product, the time you offer it, the product itself, the pricing, and many other things. Here are some ways to decide whether your idea is a good one.

Ask For Other People's Opinions

It's certainly good to get other people's opinions, but you have to be careful. Some people won't tell you what they think, others will tell you it's great when it really isn't—so you must look behind what people are saying in order to get an actual evaluation.

If somebody says, "Well, we think it's good," ask them if they will buy it—if so, why would they use it. What do they really like about it? What improvements do they suggest?

These four things will begin to give you something from which to form a fairly realistic opinion.

Compare What You Want To Do
With Similar Businesses

The first thing to do when you're about to launch a part-time enterprise is to look around and see how many similar businesses you can find. Despite the fact that we keep talking about doing

something different, it's a truism that the same old thing sells and
sells and sells. Therefore, when we're trying to make it big, we
don't go out and find something that's really unusual. We simply
try to put a little different twist on something that's already going
big.

Let's take an example: Suppose you decide to rent canoes.
Look in your phone book and see if you can find anyone else
doing it. Go talk to him. Is he enthusiastic about his sales? What
does he think of the market? Does he seem to be making money?
How many canoes does he have? Does he look prosperous? If
these answers are positive, then ask yourself if you can do it better
than he can—cheaper—do you have something that will give it a
twist?

Suppose he's advertising in the local newspaper—can you reach
more people by advertising in the high school and college papers?
If his canoes are big and bulky, would you get more business by
giving people smaller ones? If his are green, could yours be red? If
you have an idea for anything, be sure to find somebody else
doing it. Look over as many of the operations as possible and try
to get an idea of just what the business is all about.

Finally, try to come up with the idea of how to do it a little bit
better. This way you'll be in a strong competitive position when
you do start.

Try A One "Ad" Test Run

There's nothing in the world that will let you know whether or
not your new business is going over any more dramatically than to
see the results obtained from running one ad (or if your business
isn't run that way, do something equivalent to running an ad).

Let's take the canoe rental business again. Right now you don't
have a building, you don't have any canoes and you don't have
any real way to do business. Can you run an ad? Of course you
can! It would cost about $300 to buy five canoes—but you can
rent them on weekends for $7. Why not rent three just to have a
bit of stock on hand—that's $21—then place a small $10 to $20 ad
in the local newspaper, giving only your phone number. Now, sit
back and see what happens. Did you get one response? Ten?
Twenty? Thirty? . . . What? . . . Did you rent the canoes themselves?

Now, let's suppose you didn't receive any response. Assume then there's practically no market in your area. That may not be true, but then we're looking for ideas that are going to go over well, with a reasonable amount of effort. Therefore, we want those ideas that will get some response, even if we bungle the advertising a little.

If we get five responses, you can reasonably assume there is some market. After all, you only ran one ad. Nobody knew you were there.

You'll certainly get a better response when you have a permanent location and can begin to build on your own reputation. A response like this indicates a possible success.

Now, did you get 30, 40 or more calls? If so, you've probably got a whirlwind by the tail. Certainly one you can expect to get a good part-time return from. Now if you invested a total of $40 to test your idea and lost it all, you're ahead since you can stop putting in more time and money.

If you made a modest success and rented the canoes, you have your money back—and you've tested your product for nothing.

If you rented all canoes and had many calls, you not only tested your product for nothing, but now have a clear indication that you're on the right track.

How To Set Up A Sample
Product Or Idea Test

This is similar to comparing your idea with other people's businesses. It mainly consists of seeing if other businessmen would be willing to risk their money with your product or idea.

For instance, if you're offering a mail order product, go to department store buyers and ask for comments. Since every store sets aside a particular time to see salesmen, to get an appointment all you have to do is call the department store, find out the name of the buyer, then call him and ask for an interview. Since their job depends on guessing right most of the time, they make an excellent gauge. After they look over your product carefully, will they place an order? If not, why not? Is the price right? Do they like the item? What about the packaging? Tell them what you're doing and ask for an honest opinion. Don't stop when you've seen just one, but go to a minimum of five.

If you're dealing with a service, like canoes, instead of a product, ask yourself who could give you a fair test. In this case, rental operators can help. Go to a few of the biggest renting recreational equipment and see what they say. Do they think the idea is good or bad? Do they feel you'll have to put up too much money for the return? Do they think the item will be easy or hard to rent? Can they suggest some way to modify your idea to make it more workable? What else do they say?

This one method alone can be worth thousands of dollars, for it gives you a way to really test your idea without investing a penny.

How To "Consumer Test" Your Idea

It's possible you could get some terrific beginning results, yet have a product or service that just won't produce consistent sales. No matter what you do, make sure it really works under actual conditions.

Let's say you're setting up a lawn mowing service, using local high school kids. Get one of your boys and actually go out—solicit and mow a lawn. Then ask the customers what they think—Is it trimmed right? Does the lawn look good? Is the price fair?

Now stand back and ask yourself if this is the kind of job you would like on your own lawn. It is a little better than most mowing jobs. Can you make it even better? How?

Do this kind of testing with anything you're considering—canoes, mowing lawns, setting up a baby-sitting service, or anything else. Actually try it out under practical conditions. Ask as many questions as you can, then always try to add an extra ingredient that will give you a competitive edge.

How To Run A One Magazine
New Product Test

Practically every magazine has a new product department. This is simply a section where they introduce new items that might interest their readers. Getting your product reviewed here is fairly easy. All you have to do is write up a fifty word description of your item, include a picture and send it out to 15 to 200 magazines.

Let's say, for instance, you are going into the mail order business with a new kind of lawn edger. You will want to write this item up and send it to magazines with some gardening interest. This would include general interest magazines such as *Parade,* house and garden magazines like *Better Homes and Gardens,* science and mechanics magazines like *Popular Mechanics,* and business magazines (trade journals) like *Lawn Garden* and *Outdoor Living.*

You can find magazine listings in *Standard Rate and Data Service* (available in the library reference room).

At this point we're not ready to launch an all-out campaign, so don't send to more than ten or fifteen releases—just enough to insure pickup in one or two magazines. This can be done for about $20 provided you take the pictures yourself.

Try The Trade Show Test

At trade shows and fairs you get a chance to talk to potential customers in a fairly informal atmosphere. Many of them are the top buyers, who will buy a product only if they think it has real potential. By taking a booth here, you'll give yourself a real test.

For instance, one newcomer to the field took a booth at the New York Toy Fair, set up his display of a new bean game, and wrote several thousand orders in the first few hours.

The next year, introducing a new sparkling airplane, he had the opposite reaction. The buyers literally turned their backs and walked away from his display. As a result, he dropped the idea immediately.

To find the addresses of these shows, go to the library and ask for a business magazine in the field of your product (toys, lawn and garden, sports, etc.). A current issue will carry a calendar of the shows coming up. For addresses, write to the magazine—or the show itself—in care of the address listed in the calendar. "Exhibits Schedule," 1212 Chestnut Street, Philadelphia, Penn. also contains a complete trade show directory. You can also run the same type of test at your local fair for from $25 up, depending on the fair.

This applies to almost any kind of product or service. Let's suppose, for instance, you're about to start a lawn garden service. Rent a booth, make up a number of posters, get pictures of yourself in action, print brochures and provide a way for customers to sign up. One retiree, interested in this kind of service, set up a real tree in his booth, and put on an impressive spraying demonstration. The result—150 new customers, well worth the price of the booth itself.

Use This Magic Money Potential
Formula To Get Rich Fast

The final test, of course, is always how much money can you actually make from your product or service. You can't really tell ahead of time, but you can begin to get some idea.

To do this, utilize a *money product potential formula.*

For Services:

$$TPP = DPJ \ X \ NOJ - EC$$

Total Possible Potential=(Dollars per Job)
X   (Number of Jobs Possible)
minus   (Estimated Costs).

For Products:

$$TPP = DPU \ X \ EUS - EC$$

Total Possible Potential=(Dollars per Unit)
X   (Estimated Unit Sales)
minus   (Estimated Costs).

Now let's see if we can apply this to a lawn and garden spray service. You will, of course, have to estimate costs, expenses and possible times.

First, similar services do six yards per four-hour period with one man—charging $10 a month for two sprayings. Applying this monthly shows that one man working alone 24 hours a week could theoretically take in $720. Estimating $200 a month expenses for a pickup truck, spray equipment and supplies leaves $520.

Put this in the formula—$10 X 72 jobs per month—$200 = $520.

Now if this isn't enough, let's try adding a student, the same number of hours with another truck:

$$\$10 \ X \ 72 - \$392 = \$328.$$
The only difference is labor cost.

Admittedly, we're doing a lot of guessing. But you need something to work from. In practice, if your project looks feasible at this point, start a six-month trial. If you are within 65 percent of possible potential at the end of that time, continue the business. If not, better take your loss and try something else.

Use Your Own Judgment

Run as many tests as you can—apply the potential formula, then sit down and ask yourself: "Do I feel it has potential? Will it live up to my expectations? What will I have to do to really make it work? How do I really feel about it?" In the final analysis, despite the tests, you, yourself, are going to have to make the decision, and you should give yourself an honest opinion of what you actually think.

Checking On Chapter 6

In testing your ideas, do these things:
1. *Ask for other people's opinions*—this is probably the least valuable of all methods, but you can learn if you read between the lines.
2. *Compare with similar businesses*—talk to other businesses about the problems and successes they have.
3. *Run a one ad test*—before you're ready to go, take out one ad in the local newspaper and see what results you get.
4. *Set up a sample product or idea test*—this doesn't mean selling your product to the public; simply take it around and offer it for sale to stores and see what reaction you get.
5. *Consumer test your idea*—give it to someone to use, consider his reactions, and actually see if it works.
6. *Run a one magazine new product test*—send out releases to 10 to 15 magazines and see what results you get.
7. *Take your product to a trade show or fair*—trade shows and fairs can give you a good test. Actually rent a booth, set up a display and see what happens.
8. *Utilize a money potential formula*—finally, estimate the total money you might take in, subtract expenses and see what you come up with. Remember, this is theoretical.

Chapter 7

How to Develop Your Big Money Ideas

After you've come up with an idea, tested it and decided to go ahead, you'll want to start developing your project. Here is where a lot of people run into trouble.

Just how do you proceed?

Well, it isn't easy because from here on it takes action. The main thing—don't get bogged down. Just keep plugging away. If the details, at times, seem too cumbersome, fall back and solve one problem at a time. Here are some guidelines you can follow.

Lay Out A Complete Action Plan

In order to get started, you need some plan to handle the details. The easiest way is simply to lay out your whole project on a big piece of paper. If you've made a detailed enough list of steps in Chapter 5, use that one here.

For a baby-sitting service, where you intend to hire girls, your list might look like this:

1. Think through the entire business.
2. Check to see if you need a business license.
3. Make up business cards.
4. Make up bulletin board business-solicitation cards.
5. Get business phone.
6. Line up girls.
7. Check on way to pay girls.
8. Make a list of rules and regulations for your girls.
9. Put up business solicitation cards in grocery stores.

This gives you a picture of what you actually have to do to get into action. One caution—make your list as complete and as detailed as possible. If your Chapter 5 list is not complete, fill it in before you go any farther.

List Everything You Need

This is a little more complicated than just laying out an action plan. Here you must take into account all supplies and other needs.

Let's suppose you've decided to make a small bird house to sell by mail. Under *Build Birdhouses,* put down exactly what you need, like this: *Shingles,* white-pine for the sides and bottom—¼" dowling, black enamel, red enamel, nails, screws, etc. Under *make-up—stationery*—you might put letterhead, cards, envelopes. Under *advertising*—a sample ad, sample brochures, mailing lists, etc. In other words, everything that's going to go into your project so you can estimate costs later. It's important to make your list as complete as possible.

How To Line Up Your
Sources Of Supply

One stumbling block many people run into when starting a spare-time activity is just where do you find your supplies? There are many ways to go about this. Here are some:

1. *Use the classified section of your telephone book.* Simply start at one end of the yellow pages and run all the way through. You'll be surprised what you'll find listed here—for instance, a quick glance at my own phone book shows the following:

Chrome plating.
Industrial ovens and furnaces.
Ozrol, The Magician and his balloon animals.
Packings—asbestos, teflon, gaskets, etc.
Plastic supplies—fiberglass, tubes, rods, egg crates, ceiling paneling.
Pre-cast concrete parking bumpers, etc.
Quality red clay pots—1½" to 20".
Soda fountain equipment—counters, stools, carbonators, etc.
Striping pavement marking—guide posts, street and roadside signs.
Turf grass.

Wrapping paper, twine, paper bags, scotch tape, janitorial supplies, etc.
And more . . .

2. *Try the trade publications*—most business publications
   include a classified advertising section, offering many items
   and services. (As mentioned before, you can find addresses of
   over 2500 trade publications in the *Standard Rate and Data
   Service* available at the nearest library.) If you're going to
   manufacture a toy, for instance, by all means leaf through
   the classified section of a toy magazine like *Playthings.* A
   recent issue included the following: Rubber wheel tires, steel
   tubing, stencils, dolls and toy parts, white birch dowels, cut
   reeds, plastic handles, balls, pull toys, rings, industrial fast-
   eners, bells, bulbs, assembling and packaging services, crayon
   and chalk, die cutting, cords, springs and wire forms, extruded
   plastics, advertising layouts, packaging designs, catalog sheets,
   photography, retouching services, decorative nails and practically anything else you'll need.

3. *Utilize the Chamber of Commerce*—often your own Chamber
   of Commerce will have industrial listings, plus lists of products manufactured in your city. These can help you find
   people or products you need. In addition, the Chamber of
   Commerce personnel can often steer you in the right direction.

Use The Brains And Talent
Of All Potential Suppliers

Why do it yourself when there are hundreds of experts willing
to help. Your potential suppliers often are set up to help you in
many ways.

For instance, one man trying to put out a toy top spent months
worrying about how to package a 30" plastic rod along with the
top.

One day, in desperation, he called a local plastic manufacturing
company, who solved his problem in less than two minutes by
simply adapting a break-down rod they were already manufacturing.

In another case, a young man, trying to set up a part-time
janitorial service, found he was doing a terrible job cleaning

windows. He asked a janitorial supply salesman, however, who solved this problem quickly by drawing on his own knowledge.

Actually, then, you have thousands of dollars worth of free talent as near as your phone. By all means, call your potential suppliers—tell them your problem, and see if they can't help you solve it.

How To Get Help
From The Government

Did you realize the Government is eager to help you go into business? Actually, it maintains a staff of experts whose job is to turn out information.

First, there's the Department of Commerce. You can visit the Department of Commerce field offices to talk about what you want to do, as well as pick up a number of useful publications.

Second, the Small Business Administration puts out a great many management pamphlets to help you get started. Some sample titles: Starting and Managing a Small Business of Your Own; Starting and Managing a Small Vending Machine Business; Starting and Managing a Small Bookkeeping Service, and more.

Selling by mail, SSD #3, explains mail order and talks about the market, including the kinds of goods and products to choose. In addition, the Small Business Bulletins include handcraft and home products, the nursery business, mobile homes, door to door selling, store arrangement and display, woodworking shops, and more. Finally, the Small Business Administration puts on seminars locally for anyone wanting to start a new business. For additional information contact the Small Business Administration, Washington D.C.

It's also possible to get money through Federal Reserve Bank Loans, GI Business Loans, the Export-Import Bank of Washington, and the Small Business Administration. Actually, the Government puts out literally hundreds of valuable bulletins. Best bet to find out what's available is the book *How To Get $50,000 Worth Of Services Free Each Year From The U.S. Government* by E. Joseph Cossman, Frederickville, Inc., New York, or *The Encyclopedia of U.S. Government Benefits*, Wm. H. Wise & Co., Inc., Union City, New Jersey.

Find A Similar Project And
Go Through Step By Step

We've talked about this before, but now that you're looking for details, by all means call up somebody who is doing what you want to do, and see if they'll let you spend a day with them.

Take notes. See how they start their day, look at their records and watch how they handle customers and employees. In addition, ask how they get their business, how they hire employees, how they advertise, and anything else you can think of.

This one activity alone will prove invaluable because it will give you actual experience before you have to risk your own time and money.

Look At All Angles
In The Beginning

This is hard to do, but go back through your list of steps and see if you can come up with some different approaches.

For instance, in our baby-sitting service example at the beginning of this chapter, we decided to advertise on supermarket bulletin boards. At this time, take another look and list possibilities: classified ads, throw-away flyers, door to door solicitation, telephone solicitation, a call to the personnel office of large businesses, word of mouth in your neighborhood, and anything else you can think of. Finally, go over each step this way, looking at every additional possibility. This care often will help you add additional profit.

Get An Idea Of Cost

It's awfully easy at this point to get so excited that you rush into something and discover you're spending more money than you have available. Before you get very far along, sit down and decide what it's going to cost. You did some cost estimating, of course, when testing your idea, but now you must get a lot more detailed. This time try to take into account every possible expense, then add a 50 percent fudge factor.

Now, let's take some examples:

Suppose, for instance, you're going to sell that line of mail order bird houses we talked about before. What are your expenses? How much for supplies, production, packaging, shipping, office expenses, advertising, labor, and more. Simply list all you can think of, then start phoning or writing to come up with actual cost.

If you need something manufactured, use the phone book yellow pages to find possible manufacturers, then get three to four bids. This is the figure you'll use under production costs. If you're going to produce them yourself, put in a reasonable figure for your own labor.

Now, go through every item and do the actual leg work. For instance, if it's a mail order item and you're thinking of running ads in magazines, write the magazine—get their rate cards and figure actual cost.

If it's a baby-sitting service and you're going to hire girls, figure actual advertising cost, labor for the girls, stationery cost and anything else.

I can't stress enough here—don't guess!

If you need packaging, write to several manufacturers—if it's stationery, call several office supply stores—if it's printing, go to several printers and get bids. Here's the place to do some leg work—don't skimp.

When you finish, make sure you have the money to go farther, and see if it looks like your potential returns will give you adequate profit.

How To Actually Get Started
With Your Project

Now that you've gone through all the steps, you're ready to get started. Take your action plan and simply start with Step 1—do everything you can there, then go on to the next step. Again, don't skimp, make the phone calls you should make, and take care of all details now. When you hit the bottom of your list, you'll automatically be in operation.

Checking On Chapter 7

Develop your idea these ways:

1. Lay out a complete action plan on a piece of paper—include

as many steps as possible.
2. List all needs—try to include all supplies and services.
3. Line up your supply sources.
   Good Places:

   a. The telephone yellow pages.
   b. Trade journals.
   c. Local Chamber of Commerce.

4. Let potential suppliers help—suppliers often have much knowledge they will share. Simply call them and tell them what you're about to do.
5. Get help from the Government.
   Several Government agencies can help in almost any project you intend to start—for details check these books:

   How To Get $50,000 Worth Of Services Free From The U.S. Government
   The Enclyclopedia Of U.S. Government Benefits

6. Try to spend a day on a similar project—try to find something similar to what you want to do—and see if they'll let you observe a complete work day. Try to come up with as many details as possible.
7. Go back through your step list, and try to develop different possibilities at each step.
8. Cost out your project.
   From your step and supply list—call, write or go out and get actual costs.
9. Start your project by doing everything on your step list, item by item. By the time you get to the bottom, your project will have been launched.

Chapter 8

Big Money Steps to a Giant Fortune

Once you've decided on a business, the best policy is to let others do as much of the work as possible by utilizing ads, free publicity, consignment selling, the mail, the Government, and other methods.

Today, many companies stand or fall on their ability to capitalize on this selling method. They may have a product that's great, they may have the capacity to turn this product out cheaply in quantity, but if they don't utilize all selling outlets, they might as well close their doors.

How To Decide Which
Channels Are For You

Once you actually decide what your first product will be, I suggest you sit down with a pencil and paper and list every possible buyer or user of your product or service. Also list as many ways they can be reached that you can think of. Now let's go back to our baby sitting example.

One young woman, Mary Sullivan of San Francisco, a widow with two small children to raise and no money, needed a quick source of income that would also allow her to be with her children most of the time. A good business for her, she decided, would be a baby-sitting service for working mothers. But, she reasoned, these people divided themselves into different groups: suburban working mothers, student mothers, servicemen's wives, and others. Each needed a different approach.

She could contact working mothers, for instance, through

supermarket bulletin boards, employer bulletin boards, the local
newspaper, and direct mailing pieces.

Student mothers could be contacted through student employment services, college bulletin boards, college newspaper
announcements and similar sources.

Service people could be contacted through the local bases.

After deciding this, she picked out the two best approaches and
utilized them extensively. The results: All the business she could
handle almost immediately. Today, the former housewife with no
special training or abilities is doing something she really enjoys
(entertaining and caring for small children). In addition, her
income recently passed $25,000 a year and is still going up.

You can apply this approach for almost anything you want to
do.

In the mail order field, for instance, you might consider selling
through jobbers, direct to dealers, house-to-house, to organizations, by direct mail as premiums and more.

Automatic Selling Tools That Will
Propel You To A Big Money Income

Just what are selling tools? They're simply the media you use to
sell your product or service—a newspaper ad, a direct mail circular,
a letter, house-to-house call, or a bulletin board notice. All are
selling tools. The important thing, of course, is to select the right
ones for you.

In the baby-sitting example, for instance, Mary selected a
bulletin board card and a small newspaper classified ad. She could
have used a direct mail circular or a larger ad, but she felt these
weren't necessary. Large classified ads didn't seem to pull any
better than a small, well-worded ad. And a direct mail piece
seemed too expensive for the numbers used. In addition, the two
approaches she did use pulled so well, she really didn't need the
others.

To decide what selling tools you need, list all the possible ones
you can think of, then rate them *A, B,* or *C*—in line with how
effective you think they'll be. Consider primarily the cost in
relation to the return. When finished, eliminate all but the
A's—then try to come up with as many variations as possible.

With bulletin board cards, for instance, you can hand letter,
print, or scrawl your message—you can use big, medium or little

cards. You can make them plain white, blue, green, pink, or anything else.

How To Look For
Big Money Outlets

Once you get started, you'll find outlets you didn't dream existed. With the baby-sitting, for instance, Mary's ad and bulletin board card pulled a wide variety of people—suburban housewives, working mothers, Army mothers and student wives. These she expected. In addition, however, she got calls from women volunteering for duty at the local hospital, women working at their church, and others.

To find your markets, make up a list of all possible customers, then add to it as you go about your work over the next few days. Try to examine everything you run into as a possible market.

For instance, Carl Newman of Los Angeles, one man putting out a vinyl and leather restorer had, as his major market, shoe repair shops. He made a modest living from this, $7000-$10,000 a year, just enough to provide the bare necessities of life for his family, but never enough for a new car, good clothes, a vacation trip, bicycles, a color TV or any of the other luxuries of life. Then he decided to apply the method we have just described. After this, everywhere he went he kept his eyes open. During the week he played golf, drove the freeways, went to movies, walked across a college campus and more. At the end of the week he realized his product would be great for repairing golf bags, vinyl auto tops, theater seats and briefcases. Adding these new markets to the ones he already had, his personal income exploded to $50,000 plus within the next year. At this point, Carl moved his family to an $80,000 home, purchased three new cars, and bought all the children new bikes and several other luxuries that had seemed completely out of reach just a year before.

This procedure, of course, is what you must use when you reach the marketing stage for your own product or service.

How To Use Classified
Ads Effectively

If you were to make a survey of classified ad results, you'd find some receive hundreds of calls, others hardly any. The reason, experts say, is that these ads must appeal to their particular market in a very definite way. In other words, using classified ads effectively is just as complicated as any other kind of advertising.

In the first place, classified ad readers want "just the facts"—they're looking for short ads that give all necessary details rapidly. Basically, if you want them to read your ad, you must grab them in the first two words.

A good baby-sitting ad, for instance, would read: "Baby-sitting—My Home—Pick Up—Reasonable Rates." Here you hit all needs—what it is, where, how you'll get them there, and how much.

Most advertising courses teach students a simple four-step formula for writing good ads—*Attention, Interest, Desire and Action.* The average person is confronted by 1509 advertising impressions a day, so to catch their *Attention,* you must literally hit your potential customer over the head.

One of the most effective methods is to use a *'Ho-Hum' Crasher*—a short combination of words that's startling, and makes the reader sit up and take notice.

Volkswagen does this quite successfully with their series of ads, such as the VW with a flat tire and a caption reading: "Nobody's Perfect!"

For your own classified ads, at $1.00 each and up, depending on the newspaper, you might use such things as (1) *Don't Read This!—Bargain—Stop Here—Effective as a Money Tree*—and other combinations. (2) Develop an *interest*—basically tell him what you're selling. (3) Make it *desirable.* Some examples: *Custom Drapes that fit your windows perfectly* or *Expert, conscientious baby-sitting—Babies love it!—Rubber life rafts that fit your pocketbook!*

Finally, you must take action; i.e., you must ask for the order in a classified ad (keep it short)—*Come, See for Yourself!—Call Ext. 4508—Stop By Now!*

How To Find Potential
Customers By Mail

Many times you can reach your potential customers best by direct mail. This has a lot of advantages. You can mail just as many circulars as you wish, you can select your audience—and you can pinpoint the time of mailing.

How you go about finding an audience depends. You can buy mailing lists or make up your own. It's possible, of course, to obtain very specialized mailing lists: new mothers, sportsmen, pick-up owners, apartment owners and a lot more.

If you're mail ordering an item for new mothers, you'd want to rent a new mother list that covers large sections of the country. But if it's a baby-sitting service, you'd simply want to take your names from the local paper.

Similarly you, yourself, can make up lists from newly married and divorced couples by following the papers. The State Department of Motor Vehicles, in many states, provides lists of car and truck owners, new drivers and new car owners. Besides this, you'll find a tremendous selection available from mail order brokers. Here are a few:

E.L. Natwick, 932 Broadway, New York 10, New York.
James T. True Associates, 419 Fourth Ave., New York 10, N.Y.
Moseley Mail Order List Service, 38 Newberry St., Boston 16, Mass.

Besides a mailing list, you'll also need a circular. These can run from about $3.50 a hundred at a "quick print service" to $100 or more for fancier ones. Best bet: keep it simple—use lots of white space and a straightforward message.

Also, the four advertising rules apply here as much as they do for classified ads. A lawn and garden service might say, for instance: *Tired of taking care of your own lawn? Let us do it for you—mowing, trimming, spraying services—Reasonable Rates—Call 964-7582.*

For product sales, you'll need an 8 x 10 circular showing the product. Go to a local printer and ask him to help you with the mechanical details. You'll need a picture or a drawing, plus copy. On the copy state the specifics of the product—why the potential customer needs it, the main uses, and additional uses. If possible show several uses, since these are the key to your sales.

Finally, consider other distribution methods. Local teenagers, door-to-door, newspaper inserts, under car windshield wipers, and more. Often these are cheaper than direct mail, and more effective.

How To Utilize Fairs
And Shows Effectively

We've touched on local fairs, sports shows and home shows briefly before, but now you should consider how to make this media do the best possible job. First of all, as with direct mail, you'll need some sort of a brochure. Next, try to pick the best possible location. Get the floor plan from the show management in advance, and try to decide which one will give you the most traffic exposure.

Several months before the show, start working on newspaper coverage. That is, be sure to send a news release to all newspapers, TV and radio stations.

This release should tell them what you're doing and, if possible, add a new angle. Here's one put out by a young couple just starting out that worked quite well:

FOR IMMEDIATE RELEASE

How would you like to know that your baby sitter was trained for any emergency? She is, if she comes from Newman's Sitting Service, that will be having a booth at the County Fair—Aug. 6-8th.

The Newman Agency will put on an exhibit of emergency care for children and show parents exactly what should be done. Every year over 5,000 children die in home accidents—many of them while in the care of a baby sitter. Newman's provides special training on poisons, electric shock and many other home hazards. If you're at the fair, why don't you drop by our booth and say "hello."

Finally, try to be different—we keep repeating this, but it's important. There are so many booths that you literally have to reach out and pull people in. Best way—think of something unusual. Baby sitter training is good.

For additional effect, start each program with a loud siren and flashing lights.

Another approach here, put on a clown show for the kids.

How To Approach Large Chains

If it's a service you're selling, this probably isn't for you. But if it's a product, take note. Don't feel it's impossible to approach a large chain. Like other stores already discussed, buyers often set aside particular days to see salesmen, you included.

Simply call and make an appointment. Your library can help find these firms. Call the reference desk, tell the librarian what you have in mind and ask her to look up the names in her directories. After that, call the buyer and make an appointment. If you don't like phoning yourself, hire a secretarial service (under secretarial services in your phone book) to call and make the appointments for you.

How To Develop Foreign
Markets At Home

If you're selling a product at home, it's quite possible to make sales overseas without ever leaving home. How? By mail!

One large company, with no overseas experience, simply went to the local library and compiled a list of banks in leading cities of the world. They then sent a letter enclosing a sample of the product, with an explanation—they were sending this to them because they knew they had customers who might be interested. The result was many orders from interested customers who wrote directly.

In addition, the U.S. Department of Commerce furnishes an excellent open-sesame with their Trade Lists, Trade Opportunity Bulletins and World Trade Directory Reports.

They also have what is known as a Trade Contact Survey—a specialized professional service designed to locate firms in a particular country for you. The service is conducted on the spot by a foreign service officer to find a firm to meet your needs. He also gives this firm your proposal.

This report (taking about 60 days) includes marketing data, plus names and addresses of qualified prospects. If they can't find any interest, they'll tell you why. The total charge is about $50.

To apply for a world contact survey, contact your local Department of Commerce field officer. He will assist you in preparing the forms. In addition, you may write the Commercial Intelligence Division, Bureau of International Business Operations, U.S. Department of Commerce, Washington, D.C.

How To Use Others To Help
Market Your Product

You'd be surprised how this approach works. Every day you meet dozens of people, each one of them more than willing to help.

How does this work?

Let's suppose you have a window washing service, and you want to promote it.

Now, whenever you talk to someone, always drop in, "I'm starting a window washing service. If you know of anybody in need of something like this, please mention me."

In a typical case, one young man, Harold Wise, a low-paid Los Angeles factory worker who was having a hard time providing the bare necessities for his family of six on a $6700 a year salary, decided to start this kind of service to supplement his regular salary. He also decided that this method was the best way to promote his new business. He talked about it to his child's teacher, the neighbors, the local grocer, the post office clerks and door-to-door salesmen. What happened? Later that afternoon, the teacher got into a conversation about this with a parent who owned a large apartment house. The salesman talked to a banker, and the grocer mentioned it to another businessman he knew needed this service. The result: Several new customers immediately. As he continued utilizing this method, his part-time income climbed from nothing to $300 a month, then $700 and finally $1500 and more.

The more contacts you have, of course, the better. But the average person talks to many people every day (almost without realizing it). As a result, these contacts make good walking sales boards. People really like to help—so let them.

Checking On Chapter 8

1. Once you decide on a product, you must then try to sell it.
2. Start your selling procedure by making a list of all possible markets—add to this as new ones pop up.
3. Consider all possible selling tools, such as classified ads, direct mail and others. List all those you can think of, then rate them *A, B* and *C.* In the beginning, consider only the *A's*—add as many variations as you can come up with.
4. Classified ads should follow the formula: *Attention, Interest, Desire and Action.*
5. Start every direct mail by deciding on your audience. Obtain lists by making them up, by buying them from list brokers, or in some cases from state agencies.
6. Utilize fairs and shows to find markets. Consider your booth placement carefully—always send out a press release.

7. Large chains make good markets—call the buyers and set up an appointment.
8. Foreign Markets can be developed without leaving home. The U.S. Department of Commerce provides trade lists, trade opportunity bulletins, world trade directory reports. You can also get a Trade Contact Survey, which will put you in touch with foreign firms.
9. People like to help—simply tell them what you're doing and ask for help.

Chapter 9

Automatic Income Promotion Methods That Pay Off Big

Up to this point, we've been concerned with trying to find and test a possible spare-time big money-making project. Now we have to learn how to put the go-power in it—and that's where promotion comes in.

If you intend to make big money in your spare time, then you must learn to promote what you do. With a little ingenuity on your part, however, you can get results that will literally amaze you.

Some time ago Bob Beacher, a Salt Lake City retail store clerk trying to raise a family of four on less than $4500 a year, invented a new whip top toy that delighted children and looked like it would sell well provided he could let the public know about it.

Using his imagination, Bob sat down at his kitchen table for thirty minutes a day and, utilizing the methods we'll outline in this chapter, began to promote his product. The results: Thousands of dollars worth of whip-tops sold, publicity that spanned the nation and a growing business that eventually topped $300,000 a year.

How To Make And Use News Releases Effectively

We talked about using magazine news releases in Chapter 6. In this chapter we'll show you how to put them together. In the first place, you will want to use two kinds of releases—newspaper and magazine. If you're selling a product, a magazine news release will be quite effective. Make it up as outlined in Chapter 6—also see Figure 9-1.

Throwable Life Preserver
Is Self-Inflating

The odds favoring successful rescue of a drowning person are greatly improved by this new SAV-A-LIFE Rescue Ball, because it can be thrown with accuracy *much* farther and far *more* accurately than conventional life preservers.

SAV-A-LIFE was designed to fill a gap in water rescue and water safety which has long been neglected and impractical for most present life saving devices.

Most' people can't throw a life jacket or ordinary life-ring more than 20 or 30 feet, and it takes practice to place it with any accuracy. SAV-A-LIFE, about the size and shape of an indoor baseball, has good throwing weight of 9½ ounces, and can easily be thrown with accuracy up to 200 feet to cover 40 times the effective rescue area.

The unit is activated by the water entering the ball through openings, and within seconds after it hits the water the ball opens and out springs a full-size self-inflating life preserver with buoyancy enough to support a 250 lb. person. At the same time a small anchor is dropped to keep the life preserver from drifting out of reach. It is also "Rechargeable" for re-use.

The small compact size of SAV-A-LIFE makes it easy to carry or store in a boat, tackle box, beach bag, car glove compartment—trunk or many other places where other life preservers can't. Even fits most pockets, allowing those who work or play near water to have constant access to this "baseball-size" Life-Saving Device.

SAV-A-LIFE, priced at $5.95, is manufactured by INVENTORS PRODUCTS COMPANY, 4309 Edina Industrial Blvd., Minneapolis, Minnesota 55435.

**Figure 9-1. New Product Release—This
kind is extremely effective for
introducing new products.**

In addition, newspaper releases are effective for announcing activities you're handling or projects you're going into. Since your local newspaper often will pick up what you're doing, contact them with a news release any time you open business, add some employees, start a new project, or anything similar.

Bill Borden, for instance, opened a new janitorial service in a small town and solicited five of the local churches as his first clients.

He then wrote up what he was going to do and sent this to the newspaper, along with a picture. The results—excellent exposure. The rules are:

(1) State "For Immediate Release" in the upper left hand corner.

(2) Put the date in the upper right hand corner.

(3) Give the release a title. In this case, "Local Boy Opens New Service."

(4) Tell what you're doing, list the people you're working with, and anything else that might prove interesting (see Figure 9-2).

Is It A Bird? Is It A Plane? Is It Superman?
No, It's A Delta Wing, The Hot New Item In Water Skiing

The hottest new twist to water skiing is an idea put forth by Leonardo da Vinci about 500 years ago—the concept of "wings-for-man." This now takes form in the dart-shaped, delta wing kite which is breaking all records for air-borne skiers.

Standard kites have been flown in this country nearly 20 years. However, the delta wing is a recent import from Australia where, for the past two years, the Aussies have been soaring at heights usually reserved for aircraft.

The basic difference between the standard, rigid kite and the delta wing is this: A skier with a standard kite is entirely dependent upon boat driver and boat speed for his altitude; that is, he ascends and descends in relation to the speed of his tow boat and his tow line remains attached to the boat at all times.

The delta wing skier is his own "pilot." He can control his rise and descent with a base bar which is comparable to a "joy stick" in early aircraft. He can also cut himself loose, at will, for a free fall. In this maneuver he is much like a glider pilot, soaring on the wings of the wind.

"There's a world of difference between the two types of kites," according to 30-year-old Richard Johnson, Winter Haven, Fla. "With the delta wing, you're in complete control of your altitude. Once you cut loose, you can pinpoint your landing."

Johnson is a water ski instructor at his own ski school in Winter Haven. Among his former students is astronaut Allen B.

Shepperd. Johnson appears as a ski coach in a new motion picture produced by Evinrude Motors for release next spring.

Figure 9-2. A Newspaper Release—
This kind can be made up for
many different types of activities.

Using Borden's example, you can make up your own.

If you live in a community with throw-away shoppers' newspapers and a number of overlapping local newspapers, by all means send your release to the editor of every possible paper. Include your name and address so he can get back to you if there are questions.

How To Make The
Local Press Pay Off

In order to really make your activities hop, you must become known locally. To do this, you should frequently have items in your local paper. Doing this effectively requires a system. The paper won't print your name just because you want it to, but it will print it if you're doing something that creates news. In short, you have to use your imagination and invent things to do that the newspapers will want to print.

Now, here are a few rules:

(1) Do something unusual on special occasions.
(2) Make a splash at holiday time.
(3) Do something different that's appropriate with the season.
(4) Dream up a special project or activity.
(5) Do something for charity.
(6) Do something unusual or special for the community.

Now let's see how one energetic young woman used this program:

Helen Hanson, a San Francisco divorcee who was having a hard time keeping her family clothed and fed on $200 a month, began a baby-sitting service about two years ago. This service did just moderately well until last fall, when she learned how to let the newspaper work for her. After that her new business really took off.

At Christmas time, for instance, Helen got permission from the parents of the children she cared for to involve them in various worthy charitable projects. She then had her children make up baskets for the poor—the day before Christmas they delivered these baskets to the needy families in the neighborhood. Naturally, she let the newspapers know about it.

As summer approached, she held a special summer picnic for her children's families in the local park. This included a ceremony in which she gave the kids awards for little projects they had completed. Naturally, she took pictures and sent them to the local paper, along with the names of the kids who won the awards.

Next, she held a "Help The Elderly" project—a clean-up of a widow's yard near her "school." This resulted in more publicity. The kids also participated in a march for the local heart fund, and took on a project to pick up papers and trash around their neighborhood. Each time they did something, Helen sent in a news release and a picture which resulted in extra publicity and brought all the business she could use. Today, this part-time "school" brings in roughly $13,000 a year.

How To Turn Television And
Radio Into A Gold Mine

You, too, can appear on local television and radio. Many stations have interview shows that are constantly looking for guests. No matter what kind of activity you've decided to go into, there's something about it that other people will be interested in hearing about.

Milton Thomas, for instance, a low-paid Miami hotel worker, needed extra money to pay for a number of department store bills his wife had run up, and decided to start a part-time small appliance fix-it service in his home.

There wasn't anything unusual about Milton's business, but he realized that people frequently got mad when they discovered that it was often cheaper to buy a whole new small appliance than to have it repaired. To get on local radio and TV shows, Milton simply called the local radio and TV stations and asked who to contact. He then wrote each one a letter explaining he could talk about why there was a problem and what the individual homeowner could do about it. The results: He appeared on four radio stations and one TV station. The stations received several hundred calls and Milton's income jumped almost immediately from $100 a month extra to over $1000. Milton not only paid off his wife's bills in short order, but also acquired a brand new car and a $40,000 home in a nearby suburban community.

To do this yourself, pick out something you do that has universal appeal. If you started a small mail order business, you might want to stress the fact that many people today are interested in mail order, plus the ins and outs of getting started; if it's a lawn and garden service, you might talk about how homeowners should care for their lawns; if it's a re-mailing service, you might stress that hundreds of people need someone to re-mail their personal mail for them, and go into the reasons why.

Simply pick out that topic that has good general interest.

Either call or write the station directly. It's best to call first and get the names of the people you should contact. Here's a sample letter to help you get started. (See Figure 9-3)

Belt T. Thomas
888 Bilton St.
Round About, N.H.

Mr. Thomas Gibbs
Talk Around
KLTV
808 7th St.
Round About, N.H.

Dear Mr. Gibbs:

Did you know that hundreds of people have a large number of their letters re-mailed from an address miles away from their home state?

No? I'll bet your listeners didn't either. Many mailers don't want their ex-wives to know where they are—others are dodging creditors, and some are hiding out from relatives—besides this, of course, there are a thousand other reasons.

Having been in the re-mailing business for three years, I can discuss the reasons why people re-mail and cite hundreds of interesting examples.

I'm sure this would make an interesting discussion show for your listeners—if you'd like to have me come on, call me at 922-4312.

Sincerely,

_____

Belt T. Thomas

Figure 9-3

How To Create A Splash
Both Locally And Nationally

★ This isn't easy, but you can do it. The secret simply is to keep up a news release barrage to both newspapers and magazines. You must, however, be selective.

First, take your project and list ten things about it that are unique or unusual. For instance, one retiree raising earth worms, 69 year old Leo Banmore, listed these facts:

(1) Starting with 20,000 worms, you will have two million in one year.

(2) Earth worms double every two months.

(3) Eggs are contained in the ring around the neck.

(4) Earth worms can be grown in peat moss, corn meal, ground walnut shells and other media.

(5) Millions are sold each year to fishermen.

(6) The castings from the earth worms make a good fertilizer that nurseries will buy.

(7) One man has recently come up with a method to make earth worms edible.

(8) Over ten thousand people raise earth worms in the U.S.

(9) Some women sell over a million a year.

(10) You can raise over two million earth worms in about fifty feet of space.

With this list in mind, he watches the newspaper and tries to tie into community events.

The trick, he finds, is to be creative. For instance:

(1) Just before fishing season, he takes a picture of a pretty girl

digging up some worms on his "farm" and sends it to the local newspaper, with the caption: "Fishing Time Again—Pretty Anita Coleman gets set to dig up some fishing worms for the season's opener at Banmore's Worm Farm in Sacramento. On Saturday, over 50,000 local residents are expected to head for the woods and streams, many of them fishing with worms from farms like Banmore's."

(2) During Easter vacation, he hired a half dozen college kids and sent a news release to both newspapers and magazines, stressing the unusual occupations that youth can sometimes get into on part-time jobs. The result—eight newspaper and two magazine pick-ups.

(3) He wrote a short release on how to raise worms as a part-time business and sent it to 200 magazines and newspapers— this brought stories in eight newspapers and four magazines. This technique, of course, requires imagination. It isn't easy, but it can be done. Try to decide what things people would be interested in (as far as your project is concerned), tie it together with some newsworthy event and make up a release.

Promote Yourself With The
People Who Really Count

One rule that the experts in this business constantly stress: Don't promote indiscriminately, but try to "rifle" your approach. (You'll probably want to disregard this when sending out news releases, but nowhere else.) With direct mail, or any other kind of promotion, you must go directly to people who will buy.

To reach them effectively, you must first sit down and decide who your potential customers really are.

Let's take our worm farm. Banmore decided worms could be sold effectively to grocery stores, drug stores and automotive chains selling fishing tackle, plus sporting goods stores, resorts and more. He then made a list of the ten top grocery chains in the United States handling sporting goods, the twenty top sporting goods stores, large automotive chains with sporting goods departments (like Grand Auto in California and Oklahoma Tire & Supply, Tulsa, Oklahoma), and large resorts catering to fishermen. His list contained 200 names. He then sent a series of sales letters directly to the buyers of these firms. All this effort resulted in many sales.

The rules, then:

1. Decide who'll buy your product.
2. Select the top prospects.
3. Plan and launch your attack.

How To Use The Phone Effectively

Make no mistake about it, your phone is one of the best promotional tools you have. It costs no more to make it work for you than it does not to use it. In addition, it can probably bring you as much, or more, business than any other kind of promotional tool.

First, you must be systematic. Decide that you will call five prospects on a regular daily, weekly or monthly basis. In calling, be sure to do your homework. Sit down and make a list of people who could use your services or products. Decide what their needs are and how you can meet these needs. Then call and explain what you have in mind. You should, of course, always try to put an extra twist on your pitch—one that makes what you're offering especially useful to your prospect.

Now, let's see how this works:

Let's say you've developed a calculator for figuring the correct angle for such things as picture frames. You know this is an item that home craftsmen need. Since you're wholesaling this item, you decide companies selling power tools would be good prospects. These could be demonstrated in action with a power saw to produce traffic for higher ticket items.

On your list you'll include Sears, Montgomery Wards, local hardware stores selling craftsmen's tools, chains specializing in do-it-yourself for home owners, lumber yards with a power tool line, and more.

Next, say that you've noticed in the paper that a local chain specializing in home do-it-yourself items is running a power tool sale. You reason they could very well use somebody giving an actual demonstration of your item to create traffic. In contacting them, call the president or general manager—tell him what you want and ask if he can put you in touch with the person responsible for this promotion.

Second, you explain that this is a traffic building opportunity for them—that you will come in and put on the demonstration and that demonstrations like this, with all the noise and uproar, ordinarily attract attention and pull crowds.

You may not get to do it, but you have started learning to use your telephone as a promotional tool. Now keep at it—keeping the needs of your prospect in mind. Again, go to the top person first, and let him direct you to whoever can help.

Now, let's take an example on a smaller scale.

You have started a small part-time janitorial service, and you want to line up prospects. As you drive around, note the buildings going up that might be prospects for your services. In your calls, call the construction company putting up the building, ask them who's going to be responsible for its management—call them and tell them what you can do.

Again, remember their needs. If the new building has lots of glass, stress your window washing capabilities. If they're installing a special type of flooring, stress your ability to handle this. In other words, find out what they need and try to fill it.

Besides calling five new prospects regularly, you should also use the phone several other ways.

Keep the list of names and phone numbers of anyone who contacts you about business. Make up a card file of these names and regularly check back with them to see if they've obtained this service somewhere else, or if they're ready to use yours.

Let's say you're acting as a sales outlet for a particular kind of air conditioning. Over the weeks a number of people have expressed an interest in your product. What you must do is to call them back regularly, say every three or four months, and ask them if they're ready to buy now. Since you've talked to them once before, always remind them who you are, then tell them what you have to offer. The rule is to always offer something extra on each call. For instance, you can call if you have a new model—if there's a special price on some models, or something has come up you thought they would be interested in. You must, however, always include this kind of extra appeal.

People using this type of telephone promotion find they're making sales or selling their services a year after the first contact. In addition, after a period of time they're producing a steady stream of sales.

In addition to this kind of telephone activity, you can also promote with incoming calls.

A cardinal rule here is that you must always see people in person to convert telephone calls into actual sales. This is an art that requires much practice. For instance, a call comes in and somebody inquires about your prices for a lawn keeping service. You don't simply give them the price, you say: "We try to keep our prices extremely reasonable—it's probably below most others. However, there isn't any way I can give you a firm price until I can see your yard. If you like, I can come over and give you an estimate today."

You now have your foot in the door, and a chance of doing some real business.

Let's take another example—suppose you're running a small fix-it shop. You say: "A lot of times I can fix it for a very reasonable fee, but the only way I can really tell is to see your item. Why don't you come in and let me give you an accurate estimate."

The rule: Always either ask them to come in so you can give them a firm price, or offer to go out and give them an estimate in person. This way, you convert people at the other end of the phone into actual prospects.

How To Get Others
To Sell For You

Other people can really help sell for you. The trick is to know how to get them to do it.

To get people to talk about what you're doing, you, yourself, must talk about it. Whenever you get a chance, talk up your activities—show enthusiasm, and let people know it's the greatest thing you've ever done. That's all there is to it.

If you're extremely enthusiastic, people you talk to will talk to others about you—although this seems too simple a method to really work, don't underestimate it, for it will carry your name and activities further than you ever dreamed possible.

Checking On Chapter 9

Your spare-time money-making activities can be given a real boost by proper promotions. Use these methods:

1. Send out newspaper and magazine releases—newspaper

releases should include the date, a title and what you're doing.

2. Use the local press—send out a newspaper release locally:

   a. When you do something unusual or on special occasions.
   b. For holiday promotions.
   c. For seasonal activities.
   d. When you dream up a special activity.
   e. When doing something for charity.
   f. When you do something for the community.

3. Get on radio and television by picking out something in your activities that either is controversial or has special interest. Call or write the stations and ask if they'd like you as a guest.

4. List ten unusual things about your activities, tie them into things that people would like to read about, then keep up a barrage of releases.

5. Make sure your publicity reaches the people who really count.

6. Make your phone into a promotional tool. Use it to make cold calls—to call prospects you already have, and to get people to either come in or let you come out.

7. Talk up what you do with enthusiasm whenever possible. If what you do is interesting enough, people will pass it on.

Chapter 10

How to Get New Cash Fast

Need money to start a new business of your own? Don't be discouraged. In this book we emphasize starting with $5, $10, $20, $100 or more. And if you can't lay your hands on this amount you can easily borrow it. Today you'll find this kind of cash and a whole lot more available almost everywhere. And quite often if your new business is a good bet, people will practically beg you to take their money. Now let's see how you go about obtaining cash.

Make A List Of All
Possible Money Sources

You must first understand the kinds of money available. You can get trade credit, short term loans, long term loans, and equity capital. Trade credit (which is capital) comes from your suppliers, who often allow you to buy needed items from them on 30 to 90 day terms.

Short term and long term loans are self explanatory.

Equity capital, however, is different. This you do not have to repay, but obtain by selling someone a part of your business.

Make a list of all conventional sources—list all the banks that you've done business with in the past, and who might make you a loan. If you have a substantial business you can also list insurance companies which might loan on long terms, the Small Business Administration and small business investment companies.

Go through these sources first and try to obtain the money you need. If this fails, there are many other places you can get needed money. We will detail these, along with the information you need to tap them, in the remainder of this chapter.

Friends And Relatives

Without a doubt, friends and relatives are one of the best (and often overlooked) sources for small loans. Often these people are more than willing to help if you lay out what you intend to do and show them exactly why you need the money.

Try relatives first. A good idea is to make up a list of possible names, then simply work your list and see what you come up with. After that, try friends.

Buy forms at a stationery store and make up a formal agreement. Often, however, you'll want to leave the terms indeterminate, without a definite payback date. You can frequently get these loans on low monthly payments.

Don't overlook the fact that it's not necessary to get all of it from one person. If you need, say, five hundred dollars, it's easier to borrow $50 from ten people than to borrow the $500 all in one lump sum.

You Can Use Bank Charge
Cards To Get Started

More than one business has been started with the money borrowed on a bank charge card. Most bank card plans have a provision for borrowing from $150 to $250 on your signature alone. Some will advance more by special arrangement. All that's necessary is to go to a bank and ask for the money. The main drawback is that this money costs you 1½ percent a month, or 18 percent a year.

For instance, Richard Guess, owner of "Goodies" Speed Shops, San Jose, California, borrowed $250 on his BankAmericard and started what turned out to be a several million dollar a year business selling high performance "show and go" items such as custom wheels, headers, and similar merchandise to kids and others who wanted to soup up their cars. (The name "Goodies" came from the fact that he was selling the kids "goodies" to make their cars look and perform better.)

Richard put up the $250 for one month's rent and incidental expenses. The initial stock of custom steering wheels, gaskets, shifters, gauges, etc. he had originally purchased to sell from his apartment. The store itself succeeded so well that it expanded to a six store chain within two years, then branched to a warehouse distributorship serving much of central California.

How To Get Money By Mail

Do you believe it's possible to get money simply by writing for it? Of course it is! Today you'll find several hundred firms specializing in loaning money by mail. Most will loan anywhere from $150 to $1500.

To find them, get current copies of *Popular Science, Popular Mechanics, Mechanix Illustrated, Science & Mechanics* and others, and leaf through the classified ads. After looking over the ads, write for the literature and take a look at what they have to offer.

One caution—compare interest rates carefully since some are extremely high. In addition, some firms insist that you give them a second mortgage on your property before loaning money. Don't do this under any condition.

Start A Nickel And
Dime Investment Fund

Even if you don't have any money right now, you can often literally pull yourself up by your own boot straps.

Simply take all your change every day (pennies, nickels, dimes and quarters) and put it aside either in a bottle, a box or some other container. When you get enough, open a bank account. Over a period of time, this fund will become your capital source. The big problem, of course, is that it takes a long time to save much money this way. You can, however, gear your project to the amount of money you have available and let time do the rest.

How To Get A Small
Investment Group Together

Make up your mind to do one thing now. If you're determined, you can find money. If other methods fail, you can always get a small investment group together and sell them a part of your business.

Erwin Jones, for instance, had tried all possible banks to obtain capital for a small mail order business. Failing this, he decided to sell ten individuals an eighth of the business for $50 each. Within two weeks he had raised the money and was launched.

To get started, decide exactly how much of the business you're going to sell—a half, a quarter, or a sixteenth—and for how much money. For a small business (that probably won't bring back more than $10,000 the first year), you can probably sell a quarter of it for $1,000 or so. Simply make up a prospectus. That is, draw up a description of what you're going to do, how you're going to go about it, and what equipment and money you're going to need. Then draw up an agreement, giving each person a certain percentage for so much money (you probably should get a lawyer to help you with this). You can sell these ownership shares for $10, $20, $50 or anything you decide.

In selling shares, the best place to start is with your friends and work from there. Bill Dillinger, for instance, decided he would sell 100 people $20 worth of his business, and have $2,000 in working capital. First he offered it to all his friends, with only two takers. He had, however, explained the proposition carefully to each friend and told them if they had anyone they thought would be interested, to have them contact him. By the end of the week he had talked to twenty more prospects obtained from this source. Besides selling ten shares here, he also asked the new twenty to pass the information on to their friends. Within a few weeks he completely sold out.

How To Use Mortgages Effectively

Another source you can often tap effectively is second mortgages. Many banks, savings and loans and other financial institutions will give you a second mortgage on your house when they won't loan money any other way If you fail, of course, you still have to pay off that mortgage, but it is a money source.

When deciding, start with what you owe on your own home loan. Find out how much equity you have (the difference between what your house is worth and what you still owe on the first mortgage). Then go around and see how much money a financial institution will loan on the basis of a second mortgage. Start with banks, go next to savings and loans, then small loan firms, and finally, if all else fails, contact money lenders advertising under "Money To Loan" and "Real Estate Loans" in your local paper.

Advertise For Money

In some big city newspapers you'll find a number of ads listed in the classifieds under the category "Money Wanted." What you're selling, of course, is again part of your business. Decide how much you're willing to sell and run your ad. In it put briefly what you need, what your business is, and your phone number.

How To Turn Your Assets Into
Immediate Investment Money

Even if you don't have much money available to invest in a part-time project, don't let that stop you. After all, everybody has something which they can turn into immediate cash.

Look at your garage—is there an extra washing machine there, an old chair, a few dishes, or other odds and ends? Today is indeed the age of the "garage sale"—and weekly, people make hundreds of dollars selling odds and ends they want to get rid of.

To hold a garage sale, go through your house and get together everything that you think somebody else might possibly be interested in—old toys, silverware, glasses, pieces of furniture, tools, anything.

When you have this all together, put it in one room—arrange it as attractively as possible, and put prices on each piece. Now you're ready to start.

First, put up a big sign in your front yard saying "Garage Sale." Do the same thing on the traveled corners near your house. Next, advertise your garage sale in the local paper, and finally, tell everyone you come in contact with that you're having a garage sale at your house. When finished, you'll be surprised at the response and the cash you now have on hand.

Checking On Chapter 10

You will often need capital for your business operations. To obtain it, start first with conventional sources such as banks. List all possible ones.

Next, try tapping these unconventional sources:

1. *Friends and relatives:* try to keep payments here low and the pay-back of indeterminate length.

2. *Bank charge cards:* bank plans frequently lend up to $250 on your signature alone—the interest rate on this money, however, is high.

3. *Money by mail:* many magazines, like *Popular Mechanics, Popular Science, Mechanix Illustrated and others,* carry ads for money in their classified sections. Write directly to these companies for information.

4. *Nickel and dime investment funds:* put all change aside each day for future business capital. Enterprises begun this way must necessarily start small.

5. *Small investment groups:* you can sell part of your business—make up a prospectus and decide how much. Sell shares through friends first.

6. *Second mortgages:* you can obtain capital by putting a second mortgage on your house. Start with your own bank, then try other sources.

7. *Classified ads:* you can place an ad under "Money Wanted" in most newspapers. What you're selling is a part of your business.

8. *Everyday assets:* today you can turn practically anything into money. Best way to do it is with a garage sale.

Chapter II

How to Manage
Your Fortune-Making Activities

Being successful at a part-time activity—that is, being really successful—means learning to manage your affairs properly. It means handling details efficiently and promptly and also making sure that what you do undertake is profitable.

How To See The Whole Picture

One of the biggest problems every successful businessman faces is that there are so many details, it's hard to see the overall picture. It's difficult to know just what to do next, and in what order.

Milton Jones, for instance, a San Diego factory worker who was deeply in debt from caring for an invalid wife, started a small door to door landscaping service on a $200 investment and just a few hours a week spare time. Jones used his initial investment to set up a display in the back of his pickup to show prospects. The actual merchandise was shipped by mail from a nursery in the East.

Milton simply knocked on the doors of homes in new tracts and showed them how they could completely landscape their homes for $10.00 down and $10.00 a month. The first month he topped $8,000, the second $12,000. After that, however, Milton bogged down. He got so interested in related activities like making up newspaper ads, re-displaying his merchandise, writing letters thanking customers for orders, planning his office and similar chores that he just couldn't find time to make many calls. As a consequence, sales dropped off and his income dwindled to almost nothing. It was at this point that he decided he must do things in proper order. He then made up a list of everything he had to do, and made sure that a large part of each day was devoted to selling. As a result sales once more zoomed, and within a short time he was well on his way to a $100,000 year.

The first thing you must do, then, is to lay out the complete picture from beginning to end, as we did in Chapter 5, with the emphasis on the priority activities. In that chapter we wrote down the steps necessary to launch a small specialized nursery business like this:

1. Find where to put your stock
2. Buy trees
3. Find and buy necessary equipment
4. Make up soil mix
5. Pot trees
6. Water daily
7. Build some sort of shelter
8. Miscellaneous care
9. Get them ready for market
10. Contact market
11. Transport
12. Set up and sell

Once you've completed this list, divide it into infrequent activities and regular chores. Here's an example:

Infrequent Activities
1. Find where to put your stock
2. Buy trees
3. Find and buy necessary equipment
4. Make up soil mix
5. Pot trees
6. Build some sort of shelter
7. Get them ready for market
8. Contact market
9. Transport
10. Set up and sell

Regular Activities
1. Check plants and water
2. Do miscellaneous houskeeping chores
3. Work on additional sales

Lists like this actually let you see every step needed for running your part-time enterprise.

Lay Out A "Necessary Chore" Schedule

Bob Briggs of Chicago, a former low-paid bus driver who opened a small specialty advertising business so he and his wife could move out of the city and buy a place in the country for the kids to grow up in, found himself working fourteen hours a day yet accomplishing little. His problem? Bob wasn't utilizing time correctly. He would often start on a project, then sidetrack himself. If he decided he needed something like a catalog, he'd sit down immediately and write for it. If he thought of someone he should call, he'd do it. If he found an interesting magazine article, he'd read that. As a result his time got eaten up, but necessary chores didn't always get accomplished. Even though he'd been busy the entire time, he always finished each night with much left to do. At this point, he was losing money. By laying out a Necessary Chore Schedule, however, and sticking to it, all the necessary jobs got done and Bob's business jumped from $13,000 a year to over $40,000.

The secret of accomplishing something lies in deciding just what you must do in any particular week, then doing only those items.

In order for this to be practical, first make up a list of what you actually must do, look at each item and decide about how much time it will take. On your final weekly list, include only as much work as you think it's practical to accomplish that week.

Each workday morning make up another list (from your weekly list) of things you want to do that day.

Your daily list (for the specialty nursery business) might look something like this:

1. Water
2. Make a phone call to get more supplies
3. Mix up humus
4. Contact store to see if they will take trees
5. Re-pot trees

Again, estimate the time required and make sure you don't try to do more than you actually have time for.

Check Your Work Effectiveness

Practically nobody is as effective as they should be, but some individuals accomplish an awful lot more in the same period of time than others. To find out where you stand, check yourself regularly. To do this, simply keep track of yourself from the time you go to work in the morning until you stop at night.

Be completely honest. Make sure you write down the time you spend sharpening pencils, reading, talking on the phone, staring out the window, or anything else. At the end of the day, your card may look something like this:

```
9:00 to  9:15 – Drinking coffee.
9:15 to  9:30 – Working on advertising.
9:30 to  9:35 – Talking on phone.
9:35 to  9:40 – Looking at magazine.
9:40 to  9:45 – Drumming fingers on desk.
9:45 to 10:00 – Walking up and down.
10:00 to 11:00 – Wrapping items.
```

Chart yourself for several days to get an accurate estimate. At the end of each day add up the time worked and the time frittered away. At the end of the week compile a weekly total. After looking at your daily results, list the positives to concentrate on and the faults to eliminate.

Also, make sure you don't try to work every minute and include some time for thinking. In addition, give yourself coffee breaks and some slack time. In an eight hour day, however, you should achieve five productive hours. If you fall below this goal, work at eliminating wasted time.

One other thing—your phone can eat up time faster than anything else. If possible, don't take any but business calls during working hours—even here, try to say exactly what you mean and hang up.

How To Sort Out Priorities

To make money, you must continually engage in activities that bring in money. If you have a mail order business, you must find your products, write letters, advertise, package and a lot, lot more. Remember, though, every task not directly related to making sales, sending products to customers, or bringing in money must be held to a minimum.

Unfortunately, extra activities really eat into your time. In many cases, they can be eliminated entirely without reducing your total take. As a practical matter, one businessman answers every letter that's directly related to his business, with sales related ones coming first. Others get pushed back until he finds an odd moment. This sometimes irritates people, but it doesn't affect his income one bit—and he reasons that unless they bring in an extra dollar, they must wait their turn.

Finally, assign priorities to the tasks you consider essential. Rate them in descending order of importance, then work in that order.

Sixty-four-year-old Bill Adikins, an Ohio school teacher who had lost all his savings in a bad investment a couple of years before and was now faced with retirement on a small pension in a few months, hired two high school boys at $1.65 an hour for after school lawn work, then began soliciting accounts in his neighborhood. One month later, after putting in four hours a day and all day Saturdays looking for jobs, he wound up with fifteen lawns a week for each boy.

At this point Bill hired two more boys, and kept expanding until he had ten. He then added a complete lawn care watering service for people on vacations. Within two weeks he had eight boys doing this on a regular basis. At this point he bought some equipment and began spraying shrubs.

Shortly afterwards, when his employees reached twenty-two, he started training an adult manager to take over the entire business. As soon as the man started showing competence, Bill put him in charge and immediately began another business. At this point Bill was working six hours a day plus weekends, and taking in almost $6000 a month gross.

How did he know when the time had come to expand? He didn't! He simply let the business guide him. First, he expanded to take care of the accounts that started coming in. When he reached a point where he didn't want to handle any more, he began to look for related services. When these expanded satisfactorily, he considered additional sidelines. Finally, he started training a manager.

If this could be translated into rules, Rule 1 would be:

Let natural business growth take you until you're making a good profit and feel additional growth in that direction would be a burden.

Rule 2: Look around to see what complementary lines you can add.

Rule 3: Manage these until they're doing well.

Rule 4: Train somebody to take over.

Rule 5: Open a completely new unit—you can, of course, repeat this procedure over and over and over again until you've acquired an empire.

How To Double Your Productive Powers

Most executives today complain they just don't have enough time to get everything done. While the complaint may be universal, it just isn't valid.

Basically, it's not a matter of not having enough time to get things done, it's a matter of taking too long to do the jobs that we actually do. Primarily, we hang up in four areas:

1. We don't quite know what we're supposed to do.
2. We don't really have the necessary information to get the job done.
3. We duplicate our own efforts with written communications.
4. We don't use a standard procedure for handling routine jobs.

While these four rules seem simple, they're really basic. Let's look at each separately.

Not Knowing What's To Be Done

What a terrible time killer this is. Tom McHale, a recently promoted foreman in a large factory, received an assignment to come up with a method for installing new production lines and to report back with recommendations. Four weeks later, when Tom's boss called him in, Tom had accomplished nothing. The reason—he really didn't understand what was required in the first place.

This applies to all of us—if we don't have a clear picture of exactly what we're suppose to do, we can't do it. Not only must we understand the orders themselves, we must also have a pretty good picture of the entire operation and know how each part fits together.

Therefore, before you start a project, sit down and form a clear idea in your mind of exactly what you intend to do. Especially, clear up anything that seems vague.

For instance, if you intend to make up advertising copy, try to decide in advance, more or less, what you intend to do and what you'll need. This step alone will save you time.

Incomplete Information

Quite often when we start a project, we don't know enough about the subject or we need additional facts. Make sure you get all this together before you try to actually tackle the job itself. Write a letter for materials and catalogs, go to the library, call people, send for extra pamphlets or whatever. Do not start your project until you have all the necessary information. If you do, you'll simply spin gears.

Standardized Forms

Use this with repetitive letters, advertising, brochures, memos, and all other types of written communications. It's not necessary to start new every time. One thank-you letter, for instance, is pretty much like the next except for the name. For the personal touch, you can change the last paragraph. Here too, however, you can simply leave blanks.

Make up standard forms as in Figure 11-1 for letters requesting information, sales letters, availability inquires, and practically everything else. If some of the items are different, simply leave blanks.

Standardized Type of "Thank You" Letter

_____

(Date)

Mr. (or Mrs.)_____

_____

_____

   (Address)

Dear Mr. (or Mrs.) _____:

Thank you for helping us with our presentation on_____

_____. We really appreciated your taking the time to be with us.

I hope sometime in the future you'll consider doing it again.

Cordially,

_____

Figure 11-1

Routine Procedures

New procedures always waste time. After all, the more you do something, the more you can eliminate steps. In a recent study a prominent manufacturer discovered that by outlining the steps and making the job standard, he could cut almost 50 percent off daily time requirements. The reason: Employees were taking time to make decisions about what to do next. By eliminating this, he saved that time.

Primarily, decide what steps are necessary and make up a written routine. Here's a production step from a small firm producing bird houses:

1. Get the day's materials together. Check to make sure all parts are there.
2. Place sides in frame.
3. Nail on tops.
4. Nail on bottom.
5. Take out and inspect.
6. Add first spray coat.
7. Put in dryer.
8. Add second spray coat.
9. Send across the street for sanding.

This may sound oversimplified, but standardizing procedures like this keeps you from wasting time, shows you exactly what you're going to do next and speeds up the whole process.

How To Keep Your Expenses Down

Once your spare-time business starts to boom, it's awfully easy to let expenses get out of hand.

Lyle Hampton, a San Diego retail clerk who needed extra money to pay for a heart operation for his son, started a small mail order business in July and by January had more orders and money than he knew what to do with. He then moved into a fancy office building, ordered some brand new furniture, bought a new car, hired several extra people, purchased fancy stationery and committed himself to several large obligations. Three months later he found himself paying out $300 more a month than he was taking in.

This can happen easily. You must, however, wind up every month with the maximum possible left over. Here are some ways to do this:

Delay Costly Improvements

It's a temptation to improve conditions, but in order to maximize profit, don't.

Bill Baldwin of Seattle, Washington, an aircraft factory worker who simply wanted the type of life that more money would bring, started a small printing business in his garage, and at the end of six months sank in $4,000 just to fix up the interior. Since his first year only brought in $5,000, the improvements weren't justified even when stretched over several years. Unless improvements produce substantially greater sales, don't make them.

After seeing what happened the first year, Bill cut back his expenses drastically and examined every expense twice to make sure it was absolutely necessary. The result was that when his income hit $8,000 for the second year, he was able to pocket $3000 of this as extra income above and beyond all expenses.

Stretch Payments Out As Long As Possible

Keep in mind that the important thing is how much you have left each month after you've covered expenses.

John Franklin, for instance, began a small credit collection service with a $1,000 loan payable at the rate of $200 a month. His friend, Bill Bolger, borrowed the same amount with a $22 a month payback. John struggled along, not quite meeting expenses and monthly payments, and went broke the fourth month. Bill, however, put away $150 extra a month and always had money for emergencies.

Don't Hire Excess People

Once you're doing well, you'll probably want to hire more help. Don't, unless it can produce a substantial return. You'll find labor today one of your largest expenses. To keep it in line, you must do as much of the work yourself as possible.

When you do need help, consider hiring people to work at home. These people work cheaply and you do not have to pay workman's compensation and other employee expenses. (Simply consider them contract workers working for themselves.)

Bill Hamilton, for instance, a Chicago fork lift operator who started a home book mail order business on a borrowed $35, hired a young woman to work in his home office as a typist for $280 a month. But he cut this cost by two-thirds when he let her go and instead hired a typist who worked in her own home for 25¢ a page. This allowed him to put $187 a month back in his own pocket to be used in other ways.

You can obtain home workers easily through the classified section of the local papers.

Keep Looking For Other Ways To Pare Costs

It's possible to cut corners if you really try. Simply start now by being cost conscious. For instance, can you use one sheet of paper instead of two? Can you burn some of the lights less? Can you stop using your car quite so much? There are hundreds of places. Best bet—carry a notebook and jot down cost-cutting ideas as you come to them.

Another principle—always keep trying to reduce the cost of your supplies. You can buy hundreds of items at low cost if you keep alert. Look for suppliers in *Popular Mechanics, Popular Science,* and the photography magazines. *Popular Mechanics* recently, for instance, offered wholesale prices on fishing reels, rods, beads, spinners, jigs, sinker molds, feathers, rod blanks, rod parts, swivels and many other items. Another ad offered a free catalog for jewelry, premium goods, gift items, key chains, household products, toys and more. Still others offer pictures, photographic supplies, and all sorts of products needed in your business.

Finally, as a matter of practice, when the price is not firm—

always offer less than you think you should.

Jimmy Robe, a Salt Lake City school teacher who began a small building services business on an extra $100, decided to rent a small office with an asking price of $65 a month. Applying the rule, he made a $45 a month offer that was immediately snapped up. Over the years this practice has saved him well over $10,000.

How To Manage Your Profits Effectively

Profit can slip through your fingers extremely easily. As we saw in an earlier chapter, advertising agencies who geared their whole operation toward profit made money. You can do this too by simply deciding how much profit you think you should make—20 percent, 50 percent, or what? Then work backwards. For instance, if you decide on a 30 percent profit and expect to do $3,000 worth of business the first year in a part-time enterprise, you can pay out $2,100 in expenses and still make the required profit.

Manage toward this. Lay out a budget—include rent, supplies and all other expenses, and give them a dollar allocation based on $2,100. Then each month make sure you keep within your budget. Remember, anything over this cuts into your final profits.

In addition, make sure you manage the profit itself correctly. This isn't as easy as it sounds.

Jim Bently, for instance, a Kansas City sales clerk who had opened a mail order record business several years before, found he could now take out $2,000 a month profit—all for personal use. At the end of four years, Jim had no capital available for any other purpose and no expansion. But when he stopped taking out every penny for his own use and began plowing the $2000 back into the business, it began to expand almost automatically. Using this technique, he found that within a short time the business actually built to where he could once again take out $2000 for personal use and still have money left to put back into business expansion.

You should, then, manage your profit two ways—first, decide how much net you want to take in, and figure backwards to see how much you have to spend. Second, always put aside something for future expansion.

While these two rules alone seem overly simple, you'll find them both vital and both sufficient to propel you to a giant fortune.

How To Short-Cut Details

The more you short-cut, the more you accomplish, and the more money you'll make. We'll give you a few possibilities here. There are thousands more, however, so always keep a notebook and add to these as you go along.

Never Handle The Same Piece Of Paper Twice

What a time waster this is. In many offices, letters get handled four of five times before they're taken care of. Yet every time you pick up a paper twice, you waste time. Executives who pride themselves on efficiency follow the rule of looking at a letter or any other piece of paper once, then either discarding it or taking action immediately. If at all possible, follow this rule diligently.

Don't Make Unnecessary Trips

Leaving your office to get supplies, talk to someone or gather information is a time waster. If possible, pick up the phone. Consider, for instance, the time difference between calling the research librarian and asking her to look up a manufacturer's name, in preference to going down and looking it up yourself. This rule applies to almost everything. If you can't call, then write. Always, however, make writing a second choice.

Bunch Chores

It's easy to run down to the store when you need pencils, go back for stationery, go back later for envelopes, and so on. But resist the temptation! Keep a list of all needed chores and do them once a day, once a week, or once every two weeks.

Prepare For What's Coming

You'll find preparation one of your best short-cuts. If you, for instance, intend to mail out advertising material, prepare in advance. Make sure you have envelopes, mailing lists, stamps and all other needs. This rule is another must.

Cut Outside Activities To The Bone

Don't do anything during working hours that isn't directly related to making money. If you read an interesting article, for instance, or call somebody about other activities, that time is a total loss. So is the time required to get back to productive activity. Let your guiding rule here be: *Relegate all outside activity to after hours.*

Checking On Chapter 11

1. Try to see the overall picture. For complicated activities, actually lay out a list.
2. Accomplish more by using a "Necessary To Accomplish" list, both daily and weekly.
3. Check your effectiveness by charting yourself for a few days, then trying to eliminate the negatives.
4. Assign priority numbers to tasks you consider essential, then rate them in descending order.
5. Base your decision to expand on these rules:

   a. Let natural business growth carry you until it's bringing in a good profit.
   b. Find complementary lines, add and manage them until they're doing well.
   c. Find and train someone to take over when you've added all related additional sidelines possible.
   d. Start a completely new unit and turn all old business over to your manager.
   e. Keep at it until you've acquired an empire.

6. Double your productive powers by:

   a. Knowing what you must do in advance.
   b. Getting complete information.
   c. Standardizing all forms.
   d. Setting up routine procedures.

7. Keep expenses low by delaying improvements, stretching payments out, keeping employees to a minimum, and by watching for other possible expense savers.
8. Manage profit by deciding how much you want to make, then figuring back to obtain allowable expenses. Also, by putting something aside for future expansion.
9. Save working time by handling all papers just once, cutting unnecessary trips, bunching chores, adequate preparation and eliminating unnecessary activities during working hours.

Chapter 12

How to Let Others
Help You to Make a Fortune

Your individual labor always has an extremely limited potential. As any successful businessman will tell you, you can't make big money (even in a part-time business) working alone.

You can do that only by multiplying your effects many times with the help of others. After all, you've got a physical limit. You can turn out just so many units, or take care of just so many things, and these in turn bring in just so much money. To solve this problem of limited potential then, you must start thinking in terms of other people.

In the beginning, of course, you'll probably start your part-time enterprise alone and will keep at it by yourself until it's going really well. There will come a time, however, when you'll need help to increase volume significantly. Watch for these basic signs:

You get bogged down in day to day operations. This is another way of saying you can't see the forest for the trees. Bob Bishop was a low-paid bank clerk in Dallas. He had gotten deeply into debt several years earlier and was now trying to fend off a vicious collection agency. He started running a photography film "drop" in the evenings, 7:00 PM to 10:00 PM, set up on a capital of $400. His store consisted of 4' by 4' building in the middle of a neighborhood shopping center where customers dropped their exposed film for processing.

Eventually, he figured, he'd own at least six. Unfortunately the business took a little longer to get on its feet than Bob expected.

After two years of operation he found his time taken up with writing orders, ordering supplies, advertising, manning the counter, working with suppliers and other details.

At this point Bob suddenly realized what had happened. Taking stock of the fact that his part-time income still hadn't reached $4000 a year, he hired a young man to take the details off his hands and free him for overall planning.

Three months later Bob owned five units, had increased his income to $2000 a month, and had dozens of plans for future development.

You're not handling every part of your operation successfully. Let's say you start a part-time lawn and garden service and hire one high school boy to help. You're able to supervise him, make calls, handle the bookkeeping, and keep up with the advertising. But after awhile you get so busy with the other details you stop watching your employee's work carefully. If you let this go very long, the quality of your product will drop off and you'll start to lose business.

You need help, then, when you start to let something slip. This could be the work itself, the supervision, the bookkeeping, the advertising, and more.

You constantly miss deadlines. If this happens, you must first try to judge your own performance to determine just how efficient you are. If you're not doing a good job, then you must upgrade yourself. If, however, you're getting as much done as you could reasonably expect and still can't make deadlines, then you should hire help.

You just have too much to do. This is the opposite of missing deadlines. If you never finish the work load and always have a lot left over at the end of the day, you've simply overestimated your work potential. If this goes on over a very long period, you'll find you're discouraged and convinced you never accomplish anything. Before you reach this point, hire some help.

You can't, of course, hire help when you can't afford it. But you also shouldn't be afraid to reinvest your profits by hiring other people. After all, your biggest gains will come from that.

When To Put Other People In Charge

Putting others in charge, of course, frees you to make even more money. The problem is, just when do you do it? The answer: When your project is making a good profit, yet you can make more money turning some of the time-consuming details over to others while you concentrate on areas that bring even greater returns.

Bob Rudolph, a Seattle, Washington gas company employee, invested $300 and started a small plastics business weekends in his garage. Six months later Bob was grossing $3000 a month. At this point, however, he had to spend five hours every weekend answering mail, filling out forms, and handling other kinds of paperwork. At the same time he left many orders unfilled. He solved this by hiring a girl part-time to do office work, while he spent the extra time shipping orders. The first weekend he added $100 worth of volume to his business while paying out only $8.25.

Shortly after this he turned all the shipping chores over to still another part-time employee while he concentrated on the actual production. This resulted in still further dollar profits.

To decide which details to delegate to others, ask yourself:

(1) What parts of my operation can someone else do better?
(2) What parts can they handle more cheaply?

Use Experts To Increase Income

Besides saving you money, people can also help in other ways. Specialists, for instance, can often open up completely different sidelines.

Herb Bauer of Fresno, California was extremely successful in the sporting goods business. But he increased volume considerably by adding experts in other fields.

When he wanted to expand into skin diving equipment, for instance, he hired a skin diving expert and pulled enthusiasts from all over the county. The same thing occurred in the areas of skiing, firearms, and a number of others.

To do this successfully, you must find areas that have good volume possibilities, then you must hire personnel with enough knowledge to attract others or provide a skill you couldn't get any other way.

How To Recruit People For Your Fortune
Making Activities

Getting just the right people to help you increase your part-time fortune-making ability, of course, just doesn't happen; you must go after them aggressively. Here are some ways:

Keep your eyes open for people who can help you as you handle your day to day business operations. Robert Burns of New York, a taxi driver, was told he must take his thirteen-year-old daughter out of the city for medical reasons. While continuing to drive a taxi in New York, he moved his family to a smaller community and opened a small art supply store (with a borrowed $1000) to help pay for the move. During the first two months Robert noticed many of his customers talking about a local artist who was also an excellent teacher. Robert looked up the artist and talked him into coming to work to advise amateur painters and put on afternoon and evening art classes right in the store. The result: Business doubled to $1200 a month. Later, Robert discovered a young woman who specialized in picture framing. Like the artist, her know-how and craftmanship attracted people from all over the community and again increased volume considerably. Today Robert Burns nets close to $40,000 a year.

Let others know you're looking for good help. This is another variation of "let people help." People will become walking billboards for you if you'll let them. They will, of course, often send you prospects that aren't anywhere near what you want or need, but once in a while you'll find a gem.

Talk to local college teachers about the people you need. Frequently teachers have promising students who will fit your needs perfectly. Several years ago Wendell Thomas, a high school teacher in a small California town, needed extra cash to finance the college educations of five daughters. He opened a part-time (evenings and weekends) public relations firm and found he needed the services of a good writer-photographer.

Not knowing where to turn, he approached one of the journalism teachers at a nearby college and asked him if he knew anyone suitable. Within a week this teacher sent him a prospect who turned out to be almost perfect. Together they worked the business up until it grossed almost $100,000 a year. Not only was Wendell able to put all five daughters through college, but he also had enough extra cash to buy each a brand new car as well.

Watch the newspaper. This may sound silly, but it isn't. Newspapers do news items and features on interesting local people. Sometimes their specialties will be exactly what you need.

Newspaper reading paid off for 68-year-old Walter Drake. He had started a lawn garden service to support his two grandchildren after his daughter and her husband were killed in an automobile accident. When Walter read in the local newspaper about a retired irrigationist, Ralph Hopper, living nearby, he immediately telephoned Hopper. Together they developed an irrigation-service sideline for nearby orchardists on a $300 investment. Together Walter and Ralph now pull in $1000 extra each month in addition to what they were already making.

In another case a ski rental operator found and hired a ski instructor this way—and a man giving craft classes hired a local wood carver to instruct in that specialty.

Canvass special interest clubs. You'll find lots of them: model railroading clubs, antique automobile clubs, skiing clubs, rifle clubs, drama clubs, art clubs, and more. Many of these members are real specialists in their interest areas.

In one case, the owner of a part-time wholesale photo supply business discovered an expert camera repairman in one of the local camera clubs, and immediately hired the man to expand that part of the business.

Advertise for what you need. You'll find this the least efficient of all methods. But if you're considering expanding in particular directions and have specific needs, by all means use the classified section of your local paper. State specifically what you need and give a phone number so the applicant can call you.

How To Supervise Others Effectively

Your goal always should be to obtain maximum work efficiency from your people with a minimum of supervision. Here are some rules:

Establish checkpoints. Employees do not need constant supervision, but you should check them at critical points to make sure they're working efficiently. Some of these critical points are: starting time, quitting time, production goals, income goals, and quality. To supervise them effectively you should check these areas at irregular intervals.

For instance, if you have an employee running an ice cream stand weekends at a local beach, you would check to see that he's starting on time and not quitting too early. You must also check to make sure he's producing the volume you expect, and that he's keeping expenses to a minimum. In addition, you'll want to know if he's courteous, dressed acceptably, and knows how to handle himself well before the public.

You check volume and expenses by keeping accounting records. Physical items must be checked in person. Get there yourself at opening time and see if he's on the job. Do the same thing at quitting time. In addition, observe as many other details as possible. Also make yourself extremely conspicuous and let your employee know these details are important.

Let employees know exactly how they're doing. If your employee does a good job, tell him. Praise often makes people work better.

If he isn't doing a good job tell him that also, but make sure he knows exactly what you want him to do to improve. When his performance gets better make sure he knows you're satisfied. If he doesn't come up to your standards within a reasonable time, give him notice and hire someone else for that particular position.

Encourage employees to suggest improvements. Let your people know you are open to new and better ways to do the job and that you always want suggestions. This will keep employees seeking to improve performance.

Give your employees credit when due. Giving credit, while not exactly supervision, does help increase efficiency. Make sure your employee knows you appreciate what he's doing. Make sure also that your other employees know when you feel a particular person is doing an outstanding job. Finally, talk your employee's real accomplishments up to the general public as often as possible. This simple policy will repay you many times.

Make Up A Written Policy

People do better if they know what's expected and exactly how it should be done. You can explain orally, but often something gets lost between the time you tell the person what your policy is and he's called on to perform. That's why practically every big business has a written policy that outlines how to handle the details.

You can make this written policy pretty general, but it should also include some specific details. If you're selling a product, for instance, you should include instructions on how to handle returns, how to treat customer discounts, what kind of guarantee you give, and more. Include here any forms you're going to use and all other necessary information.

How To Get Double And Triple Work

If you go about it systematically, you can increase the output of those working for you to a far greater extent than you ever dreamed possible.

First, you must set up both production and time goals. Bill Thompson found that out quickly. Bill had been a low-paid California auto production worker before he started a mail order business on $100 of borrowed capital, after his wife went on a spending spree that left him almost $10,000 in debt. Bill hired a retiree to put together bird houses three hours a day, five days a week for $1.65 an hour, but the old man seemed to take too long to finish each bird house. Bill discovered the man turned out almost twice the quantity when he was told exactly how many Bill expected to be finished each week. After that, whenever Bill hired an employee he gave that person exact time production goals. These he made low enough so almost anyone willing to work could reach them. Production using this technique, he estimated, was almost double that of any other method. Today, Bill has not only paid off the $10,000 debt but takes in almost $20,000 a year from the bird houses alone, and has launched several other businesses which are currently netting him an additional $10,000.

Besides setting goals, you can increase production by *combining steps, eliminating steps, simplifying steps,* or by *changing the steps to make the job easier.*

Using the step combining method, Joyce Hamilton, a school teacher, who began a direct mail service weekends on a $50 nestegg, found she could speed up the job of stuffing envelopes with two different mailers by combining the two into one and printing both sides on the same piece of paper.

Using the step elimination method, a mail order nursery cut their labor in half by planting trees directly in the mailing container instead of an intermediate planting box.

Using the step simplification method, Bill Raines, a San Francisco florist's helper who started a part-time mail order business evenings, cut labor effectively by folding his mailing pieces once instead of three times and stuffing in a larger envelope.

And using the step changing method, Bill Brier, a Colorado factory worker who opened a group of three roadside fruit stands which he operated weekends, changed his method of loading his trucks at random and began loading them according to the boxes coming off at each stand. This cut delivery time almost thirty minutes, resulting in considerable dollar savings at the end of each month.

Finally, you can get more work from people by making sure they have a clear understanding of what they're doing and by making them feel you're giving them complete responsibility for their work area.

Thor Hayden, an Ohio tire factory worker, ran a small lawn sprinkler business part-time evenings and weekends on a $50 loan from his mother, Thor hired two college boys at $1.80 an hour to assemble the final sprinkler head. Three days after Thor hired them, however, they'd only finished five. Even though he'd gone through the method five times, Thor found out the boys still didn't quite understand how to put the head together. He explained once more, and this time made them do several while he watched. When they became perfect at it, he put them on their own. The results—considerably increased production and an extra $7000 a year for Thor.

Later, he told these same two boys he was making them responsible for the complete production of the sprinkler head, that nobody could tell them how to do it any more, but that he expected them to take charge and try to increase production as much as possible. As a result these boys made three simple changes the first week and took great pride in the fact that the heads were now coming out faster than the other workers could assemble the finished sprinkler.

Know When To Hire It Done

Doing the work yourself or having employees do it is not always the cheapest, most efficient method of getting a job done. You should, however, learn when to take a different approach.

Hire it done when someone else can do the job better at the same cost. Dodd Hilton, a Pacific Northwest aircraft factory worker, started with $75 and put together an informational booklet mail order business for travel trailer owners when he needed extra money to pay for hospital bills for his son who was injured in a high school football accident. In the beginning he handled the entire layout, got his copy camera ready, designed the booklet and had it run off by a local printer.

One day the printer said to him that if he'd just give him the copy and tell him what he wanted, he could do all the steps for only $100 more.

They sat down and figured it out, and Dodd said go ahead. The finished copy looked much better, cost only slightly more, and left him considerable time to work on the other projects. Result: Dodd now makes $17,000 a year more with half the effort.

Hire it done when someone else can do it cheaper. Greg Randolph, a Portland, Oregon schoolteacher who ran a small part-time mail order firm weekends so he and his wife could finance some fancy vacation trips, had his employees take pictures of all products at a cost of about $30 each.

While ordering some other material he discovered, however, that a nearby firm could do this product photography at a 30 percent savings. Gregg simply turned the entire photography operation over to them and put the savings back in the business, which brought him an extra $11,000 a year in addition to his $10,000 a year salary.

Hire it done if you can get more expertise at the same cost. Milton Boggs, a Denver, Colorado government worker who dreamed of buying a fancy home in the suburbs, ran a small part-time lawn and garden service weekends (with a shrubbery-spray sideline.) In the beginning Milton employed a high school boy to do the spraying for about $250 a month, but soon discovered that for the same cost he could hire a separate firm with a trained horticulturist. This resulted in a far better job, many additional referrals and increased volume to almost $2000 a month.

Hire it done when you can make a profit on the additional service. A young Pittsburgh woman schoolteacher with six children to support and not enough money to do it started making custom clothes for local women (weekends) and soon built the business to $1000 a month gross. In the beginning she handled the reweaving jobs herself, but soon gave this up and sent the work out to an expert. For this service she charged the customer her cost plus a 40 percent profit. This resulted in a greater dollar return for the time spent than she could get any other way, and an extra $3000 a year in addition to her regular business income.

How To Get Other People To Help

Getting other people to pitch in and help is as simple as ABC. It's simply a matter of knowing how to go about it. Actually, people really like to help when they feel you need them and consider their experience important.

Art Rouse, Editor and Publisher of Trailer Life magazine, is a past master of this technique. In one case, Art indicated to a number of people that he was starting a new houseboating magazine and since he wasn't an expert in the field, he really needed help in laying out editorial direction. One person receiving this request spent a good many hours getting together a complete format (free) which later became the basis for the first issue and many subsequent ones.

Art at one time also indicated that he was looking for land to start a "Houseboating Park," and would like people to keep their eyes open. The result: Many individuals all over the country went around looking for a place to start his "park."

The secret: Simply indicate they can do it better than you can (which they can in many cases), that you really need help, and that you'd appreciate anything they can do.

How To Use The Incentive System Effectively

You'll find the incentive system an extremely effective supervisory tool since it really motivates people. You can give incentives two ways: *in terms of responsibility,* and *in terms of money.*

In terms of responsibility, people work better the more you show your appreciation for what they're doing. Basically, the better one of your employees performs, the more responsibility you should give him. Put him in charge of another employee, another operation, or a complete section of your business enterprises. This is in itself an incentive, and will encourage your people to do their best.

Besides this, you can offer money. Don't give large amounts, but consider regular raises, small bonuses, percentage of profit increases.

An employee doing a good job must receive regular increases if you expect him to continue performing satisfactorily. This simply indicates he's doing a good job and you appreciate him.

In addition, if an employee does especially well, consider giving a bonus. If your part-time business involves selling, give a bonus for reaching certain quotas. You can also apply this to piece work, office work, or anything which involves turning out a certain amount of work daily.

Regardless of whether you can measure results, however, good work always deserves a bonus reward. If you announce these in advance, you'll find your employees working toward them.

Besides this, consider using the percentage system. Some part-time executives offer their salesmen and others producing a direct income return, a percentage of anything over a fixed base. This, they find, encourages their employees to keep increasing dollar volume.

Other people, you'll find as you go along, can be important to your business. They can effectively increase your volume and multiply your own efforts considerably.

Checking On Chapter 12

Every person has a physical limit. To increase your potential you must start thinking in terms of other people.

To determine whether or not you need help, watch for these signs:

1. You get bogged down in day to day operations.
2. You're not handling every part of your operation success-fully.
3. You constantly miss deadlines.
4. You have too much to do.

Put other people in charge when your project is making a good profit, yet volume can be increased by turning the time-consuming details over to others.

Hire experts when you need additional expertise in order to expand in specialized areas.

You must go after good people agressively. Here are some ways to find them:

1. Keep your eyes open as you conduct everyday business operations
2. Let others know you're looking for good help

3. Talk to local college teachers
4. Watch the newspaper
5. Check with special interest clubs
6. Advertise for people

You should supervise your people by *establishing quality checks,* by *letting employees know exactly how they're doing,* by *encouraging suggestions,* and by *giving credit when due.*

Make up written guidelines for your employees. Big business always uses written policy—you should too.

Increase work volume by *combining steps, eliminating steps, simplifying steps,* and by *changing the steps to make the job easier.*

Hire particular jobs done instead of doing them yourself when:

1. Someone else can do the job better at the same cost.
2. Someone else can do it cheaper.
3. You can get more expertise at the same cost.
4. You can make a profit on the additional service.

Get other people to help you by letting them know they can do it better than you can, that you really need help, and that you'd appreciate anything they could do.

Use the incentive system by giving employees more responsibility and money for better work.

Use: regular raises, bonuses, percentage of profit increases.

Chapter 13

How to Pyramid
Your Fortune-Making Activities

You can make good money from a single spare-time enterprise, but you'll probably never get rich that way. Making big money with the spare-time route, really big money, requires a completely different approach, and that's where pyramiding comes in.

Pyramiding is simply multiplying the effectiveness of what you're doing many times by using assets already available. It does not mean starting a new business, or a new aspect of the same business. It does mean getting the absolute maximum out of what you're already doing.

For example, suppose you build a canoe rental business to a $3000 a month gross, then decide you can sell canoes also. You put up a sign "Canoes For Sale," talk sales with every customer and allow him a percentage of his rental toward the purchase price. By the end of the month you've added an extra $1000 simply by taking advantage of the rental momentum you've already created.

This, in effect, is pyramiding. To do it effectively, you start with what you have and expand. In this chapter we'll show you how to do it effectively.

Set Up An Idea Board

A few years ago Noel Carpenter, a $600 a month candle factory worker supporting his elderly parents, suddenly found he needed an extra $150 every month to help them purchase a new house.

First he tried to borrow the money, but nobody would loan it to him for that purpose. Finally, he took the $300 savings he had accumulated painfully over the last ten years, purchased some almost new skis he found in a classified newspaper ad, rented a $35 a month store and opened a ski rental business four days a week (Thursday and Friday evenings, and all day Saturday and Sunday). Rentals went so well as a result of a small ad run in a local college paper that Noel immediately ordered a new ski inventory and launched into sales. After that he sponsored a ski club, which resulted in more business.

Next, Noel set up an artificial hill, hired an instructor and offered lessons and rentals at a package price. He then launched ski trips to nearby ski areas. By this time he had six part-time employees and a $9000 a month income. He then went out and bought his parents a brand new $45,000 home, a new car, and sent them on a six week trip to Hawaii.

How did he come up with these pyramiding ideas that zoomed his income? All came through the use of an idea board. This is simply a large 5' by 7' board placed on the office wall and devoted strictly to pyramiding ideas.

These ideas he found by going through the local newspaper regularly and clipping out any possible item. He does the same with six different magazines. In addition, he keeps a notebook to jot down ideas as he finds them. Anything that triggers him while watching television, driving down the street, having lunch or anything else, gets placed in the notebook and stuck on the idea board. In the course of a month this board accumulates forty to fifty possible pyramiding ideas.

How To Operate An Idea Board

First, you must keep ideas pouring in—and this means keeping alert. When you take a walk, listen to a speech, watch television, eat lunch or any other activity, jot down anything that seems remotely promising.

Collect as many as possible. You won't use everything you place on your board, but you must have a wide selection of material when you start your actual weeding process. Pay no attention to how silly any one idea might seem. Properly reworked, these may turn out to be your best.

At the end of each month, go through and weed your board. Discard anything that just doesn't fit. Go through the rest and try to combine or modify.

Let's say, for instance, that you shoe horses part-time for local horse fanciers. Some of the ideas you find on your board at the end of the month are:

> Sell a related line of medicines
> Offer trail rides
> Offer a boarding service
> Sell saddles
> Sell feed
> Rent horses weekends
> Offer saddle blankets
> Offer accessory items

You can combine saddles, saddle blankets, and accessories. You can eliminate horse rentals, trail rides, and boarding services as impractical unless you already have the facilities.

This leaves selling saddles, blankets, feed, chemicals, medicines, and horse accessories. Go through these (and anything else that's left) and try to add a twist.

For instance, if you have a panel truck for your business, you might try turning it into a traveling salesroom by displaying saddles, blankets, and accessory items along one side.

With medicines, you might print a list and hand it out to your present customers. For feed, you could rent a trailer, load on some bales of hay and sell them wherever you go.

How To Decide Which Projects Will Pyramid Your Income

You must now try to decide which projects will really pyramid your efforts and which will result in more work than they're worth. To do this we must start utilizing the principle of using the interest from your activities to make more money, not the principal of the activity itself. This means utilizing the potential you've already created in building your first activity rather than starting all over again.

Let's say you're now operating a successful part-time private campground. You've found a location, laid out the sites, built roads, and in short completed all the hard work. Now campers come regularly and bring you a good income. That's great. This initial work is your principal.

If you start another campground, you must naturally go through the entire process again. That's not at all necessary, however. You can now add to your income without doing any additional basic work.

Suppose, for instance, you originally built a small campground entrance house. You now open up a back room, put in shelves at a cost of about $300, and add a small stock of groceries and accessory camping items. Suddenly, with very little effort, you're making more money.

You then ask the nearest big town newspaper to send you a rack and 100 newspapers every day. The result—even more income. After that you buy a movie projector, put up a screen, build some log benches and show evening movies for $1.50 apiece.

Finally you dig out a little creek that runs through the campground for about $350, fill it with trout, buy some fishing poles and bait, and charge for the privilege of pulling out rainbow trout. Every one of these activities brings in extra income, yet every dollar comes from customers you've already brought into your campground. You do not have to do major groundwork to build a market. You did that in the beginning.

Pyramiding occurs then when you use the market you've already built to create new income. It's simply a practical application of the rule, *use the interest, not the principal of your activity.*

How do you decide when you can do this? Ask yourself these basic questions:

Does my new project tie directly to the old one? That is, is it a natural outgrowth of what you're already doing? If not, avoid it.

Can I start the new project with minimum capital? If you need to invest a large sum, you're not applying the rule properly. You should have already made the major investment, both in time and money.

Is my market already there? That is, have you already built customers for the new activity? You created customers for your campground store, for instance, by building the campground in the first place. After all, all campers need extra groceries.

Can I keep the new operating costs low? Pyramiding falls down when the new project overhead rises. You can operate your camp grocery store, for instance, with the same people who handle your entrance gate. Outside of the money needed to remodel the entrance house and stock it, you can get by with almost nothing extra.

Now apply these questions to your own pryamiding projects and see how they stack up. If you can answer "yes" to each one, you have a project that will pyramid effectively.

How To Put A Pyramiding Plan Into Effect

Exactly how do you get started pyramiding? This is an application of what we've done several times before. Go back to your pyramiding board, take down a project you intend to work on and list all possible steps needed to get you into action.

Let's look at the campground example again. Say you intend to add the trout fishing pond. First we'll list all steps necessary to go from bare ground to finished fishing pond. They might look like this:

1. Decide on a spot
2. Get estimates on a dam
3. Hire the job done
4. Find out where to buy fish
5. Buy them
6. Put up a bait shack
7. Find out where to get bait and poles—buy both
8. Put in fish and set up signs.

Now set aside thirty minutes every day to actually work these steps. It's as simple as beginning at the top and working to the bottom. Do as much each day as you can, being regular and systematic. This system cannot help but launch you into action.

How To Use Spin-Offs

Spin-offs, of course, employ the old principle of using the interest instead of the principal. Spin-offs, as we've said before, are not new projects, but outgrowths of what you're already doing. If you're renting canoes, for instance, sales are outgrowths; so are accessory rentals. Now, to obtain maximum results you should constantly try to keep increasing your income from each spin-off. How? Here are some rules:

Try to find other ways to merchandise what you're doing. Take canoes again. First, as we've seen, you can rent them in the conventional way. You might also try a rent-to-own plan, a canoe lay-away, guided canoe trips, rent-a-canoe "at the lake of your choice" plan and many, many more.

Simply try to think up as many ways to merchandise your product or service as possible. Each new method means extra cash.

Let's take another example. Say you're selling jam at an outdoor stand. Different methods of merchandising would be direct sales to stores, gift packaging, jam of the month packages, a gourmet jam club, mail order and more.

Use in-operation signs. It's an old axiom that you can't sell anything—services or products—unless you advertise. This doesn't have to mean ads in newspapers, radio, television, etc. Once you have generated the traffic all you need to do is tell the people who visit you or already buy from you what else you have to offer.

Simply set up signs. You can handletter or have them printed, but for greatest effect use bold letters and striking color. List the additional services or products you offer plus the basic features and price.

Set up displays. If you can display your spin-off, do it. One part-timer selling jams at a roadside stand set up a huge display of gift jams in fancy boxes. The result—hundreds of extra dollars.

If you're selling a product, set up a display—if it's a service, use a graphic representation of what you're doing. Two Colorado teachers running a four hour a day summer play program for small children set up a tent, and simulated a campfire and a mountain scene to demonstrate how they took kids on camping trips during the month of August.

Talk it up. In addition to signs and displays, you can sell an awful lot of things by talking about them. Retailers learned long ago that they can double the volume they're doing on particular items by simply talking about them with every customer. You, too, should become a walking billboard.

If you operate a part-time baby-sitting service, for instance, and you also teach remedial reading, be sure to mention it every time you open your mouth. You'll be surprised at the number of customers you'll gain this way.

How To Manage Multiple Projects

The first rule: Manage each project separately. Bill Jennifer, an airline employee with mornings off, rapidly built $500 and an old van into a three-truck coffee and sandwich operation grossing $60,000 a year. After this success, Bill opened an equipment rental service in a minority group neighborhood. He tried to handle the two businesses together, but failed to watch the rental operation closely enough. As a result, he didn't advertise at the proper times, didn't add new items when needed, and didn't make sure his customers were getting good service. At the end of the next year he found himself in deep trouble and had to fight to just barely hang on.

Since Bill wanted to specialize in home repair, sick room supplies such as wheel chairs and crutches, and exercise equipment, he should have first decided what inventory he needed and what volume he wanted. He then should have set up his promotional programs and advertising schedule, checking regularly to see that everything was going all right. Next, he should have checked to see that the operation was making the expected volume. If not, he should have then sat down and decided what was wrong and what was needed. If, on the other hand, he was making his first goals as expected, he should have then begun getting ready for the second.

To spell it out: Lay out tentative goals—decide what steps are needed to reach that first goal. Start and complete each. When it looks like you'll reach one goal, lay out a detailed plan for reaching the next. If you fall down somewhere, go back and try to determine what changes are needed. Make them and go ahead. Check regularly to make sure you're proceeding on schedule.

Systematic handling of each project as a separate entity like this will launch each smoothly and keep the entire operation running without a hitch.

How To Use A Three
Step Actionizing Plan

Spinning off activities is as simple as A B C, if you follow the formula known as the "think," "talk," "action" plan.

First, let's say you have the canoe rental we keep talking about set up and going, and you decide to supplement this during the winter with a complete ski rental program.

To put the plan into action simply start thinking in detail about what you're going to do—think about the inventory you'll need, consider the type of remodeling you must do, picture your new fixtures, go over the advertising in your mind, and consider what would happen if you started running ski buses.

Next, start talking about the project with anyone who'll listen—discuss it with your wife or husband. Tell them what you're doing now, and how you're going to start the ski rental business. Go into as much detail as you can. Encourage them to ask questions. This will help crystallize the idea in your own mind—and until you can convince yourself you can put something into operation, you probably can't.

Once you've become convinced through thought and talk, sit down as we've done before and make up your action list of needed details. As before, start with step one and work all the way through.

While extremely simple, the three step "think" "talk" "action" plan will get you so fired up, you just can't miss.

Harry Smith, a San Francisco paint factory worker, uses this plan quite effectively. An extremely energetic individual, Harry previously launched a $9,000-a-year coin-op laundry operation on a $300 nest egg, and has recently opened an amusement pinball machine and "dodge 'em" car concession between a miniature golf course and a drive-in movie.

Before he ventured into the recreation field, Harry thought over the details for a long time. He knew about a perfect building with a lot in back for the "dodge 'em" setup. He imagined dickering to rent the building, contracting for the alterations, buying the equipment, putting it in and more. He saw it finished in his mind and the crowds of kids pouring in.

He then talked over all the details with his wife. She offered a number of suggestions which they discussed completely. By this time he could see the project clearly and knew exactly what he had to do. He then made a list and started at the top. From then on the business literally opened itself, and today brings him an additional $9000 per season with practically a whole year left to enjoy it.

How To Manage For Impact

If you expect your potential customers to know you're there you must create an impression. Surprisingly though, this impression doesn't depend so much on advertising as it does on what you actually do.

Here are some of the ways you can create an impact:

Talk it up a lot. You'd be surprised how important this is. The more you talk to people and get them to talk to others about you, the more impact you have.

George Clampton, a Columbus, Ohio variety store salesman, was in desperate need of an extra $200 a month to hold off a threatening collection agency. He could have borrowed the money, but that would only have taken him from the frying pan into the fire. Instead, he begged a hundred dollars from one of his friends and launched a part-time rubber stamp business.

The first thing he did was to tell all his friends what he intended to do and ask them to tell anyone they thought might be interested.

Next, he mentioned it to anyone else who would listen. Sunday he told his pastor and twelve other church members. During the rest of that week he told sales clerks, business acquaintances and a number of people at several meetings. All received a card listing his name, address, and the fact that he made rubber stamps. By the end of the second week he had received fifteen telephone inquiries, none from complete strangers, all as a result of talking impact. Today George has an automatic $12,000 a year part-time business and a savings nest egg of almost $30,000.

Make a visual impression. You can do this in several ways. John Hollstrup, a Seattle, Washington bus driver, created a ten hour a week, $1000 a month part-time business selling plastic slap-on car signs. Then he got the bright idea of increasing the business with visual impact. From a local printer, he ordered 500 bumper stickers for $55 saying "TO GET YOUR SLAP-ON PLASTIC CAR SIGNS call John 928-4766." He offered all car sign customers a slight discount to put these stickers on their bumpers. He installed them on his own car and talked as many friends as possible into doing the same thing. Two months and 410 stickers later, people all over town knew exactly where to buy their plastic car signs, and John had almost doubled his monthly part-time income.

Reggie Reynolds needed extra cash to pay off a hospital bill. He was a department store shoe salesman, but decided to go into part-time business for himself selling mail order shoes directly to local businesses. Clipping an ad from a popular magazine, he sent for the brochures, then ordered a few sample shoes and a regular sales kit. After this he constructed five large six-foot plywood sandwich signs which said, in four-foot letters, "See Reggie Reynolds for Shoes." These he mounted on six small trailers which (with permission of the owners) he parked all over town in shopping center parking lots.

After that, whenever he entered a store and announced his name was Reggie Reynolds, someone would invariably say, "Oh, you're the guy with the signs all over town." The fact that they already knew and recognized his name always made his selling job that much easier, and brought him a $25,000 a year income he'd once thought completely out of his reach.

Make an impression with the telephone. As we mentioned before, every call coming into your house gives you an excellent opportunity to sell. Take it. Talk about what you're doing whenever you get the opportunity. If possible, even ask for the sale over the phone. You'll be surprised how effective this is.

Besides this, keep a notebook and list additional ways to make an impact as you come across them. Also keep looking for variations or unusual applications of the three impact methods listed here.

For instance, you might want to put up posters on the sides of buildings, go door to door shaking hands, or walk up and down in front of your house carrying a sign. There are dozens of ways. You will need, however, to select the ones you feel are most effective for your enterprise.

Finally—repeat, repeat, repeat. To really create an impact you must use constant repetition. Simply use the three methods above in as imaginative a way as you can, over and over and over again. Never underestimate the importance of repetition, but use it consistently to really create an impact.

How To Make Sure All Projects
Complement Each Other

Make sure all projects fit together effectively. This means they should all lie in the same interest area. In our canoe example, for instance, sales fit with rentals and such items as cushion rentals, canoe trips, and rentals in outlying areas all fall in the same interest range.

In addition to this, ask yourself, are these things (that I want to go into) natural off-shoots? That is, does the market for your first activity almost automatically become a market for the new activity?

With the canoe rentals, people were asking for life jackets long before they were available. And almost automatically, a customer for a canoe also became a life-jacket customer. You must apply this principle to everything you do if you expect the projects to all complement each other and really become successful.

Make sure, however, that you do not have to generate additional traffic or customers for any new project. They should, as we've seen before, already be there. If they aren't , discard that idea and go on to the next.

Checking On Chapter 13

You can make big money from a spare-time enterprise by pyramiding. This means getting the absolute maximum out of what you're already doing. Here are some ways:

1. Set up an idea board. Simply put everything you can think of on the board that will give you additional income from what you're already doing.
2. Regularly go over your idea board. Weed out ideas and try to put a twist on those left.
3. Always use the interest of what you're doing, not the principle. Let what you're doing now create your next enterprise and supply the customers for it.

Decide when you can do this by asking these basic questions:

   a. Is my new project a natural outgrowth of what I'm already doing?
   b. Can I start the new project with minimum capital?
   c. Is my market already there?
   d. Can I keep the new operating costs low?

4. Put a pyramiding plan into effect by listing necessary steps and starting at the top.
5. Use spin-offs effectively by:

   a. Trying to find other ways to merchandise what you're already doing.

b. Setting up signs that call attention to your new enterprises.

c. Setting up displays that show off the activity.

d. Talking about the new things you're doing.

Manage multiple pyramiding projects by laying out tentative goals, deciding on the steps needed to reach the first goal, and completing each. When it looks like you'll reach that goal, lay out a detailed plan for reaching the next. If you fall down, go back and start again. Check regularly to make sure you're proceeding on schedule.

Put pyramiding plans into action with the "think," "talk," "action" plan. That means think about what you're doing in detail, talk about it as much as possible, then do it.

Manage for impact by:

1. Talking about your enterprise a lot
2. Using visual impact whenever possible
3. Taking advantage of incoming telephone calls to talk your enterprise up

Try to be as imaginative as possible with these three and repeat, repeat, repeat.

Make sure all projects complement each other by making sure all lie in the same area of interest, one automatically supplies customers for the other, and that you do not start any project that requires you to generate new traffic or customers.

Chapter 14

How Records Increase Your Profits

Records really are the lifeblood of your part-time business and should be kept regularly. They should not, however, be complicated, nor should they take time away from your other activities. Good records are simple and easy to keep with minimum effort. This chapter will show you how to set up this kind of record and make it work for you effectively.

Knowing Where You Stand

Records increase your profits primarily by letting you know where you stand. They tell you which activities to emphasize and which to eliminate. They also tell you how much business you're doing, how much cash you have on hand, how much money you owe other people, how much your expenses are, and how much profit you're making. In addition they let you know the trends, how you're progressing, and when something starts to go wrong.

How To Set Up Simple Books

The easiest system to set up and maintain is a cash system. You can, of course, make your records elaborate and complicated, but unless you have plenty of time to spend on this one activity, don't do it. Keep records to one page, and try to include just the entries you'll need to do business effectively.

Include sales or money taken in, your "draw," inventory purchases, supplies, meals and travel expenses, gasoline, automobile expenses, insurance, postage, advertising, wages, professional services, miscellaneous expenses and any categories needed to handle your particular business. (See Figure 14-1)

One more point—draw (the amount you pay yourself) is not considered by bookkeeping standards to be an expense, but part of your profit. In a small (or even large) spare-time enterprise, this is difficult to handle from an operating standpoint. To make it simple, we are violating bookkeeping rules here and are considering this item an expense.

In addition, to simplify handling, put all money received into your checking account and write a check for all expenses. In your records enter either deposits or checks, nothing else. (See Figure 14-2)

For small amounts, write a check for Petty Cash in the amount of $10, $15, $20, etc. After that, keep receipts and when you need cash for small items, add your receipts, attach them to a petty cash slip and write a check for that amount. (See Figure 14-3)

How To Figure A Profit and Loss Statement

A profit and loss statement tells you whether you're making money or losing it, and exactly how much. Without a doubt it's one of the most important tools in your business, since it allows you to see exactly how you're doing and also lays out your expenses in profile.

A business profit and loss statement can be complicated. However, since the majority of our efforts in a spare-time business must be directed toward the business itself, it's important to keep your profit and loss computations extremely simple. You will need to know your gross profit for the month, the cost of any inventory, and your operating expenses—that's all.

If you're selling merchandise, you'll subtract the cost of that merchandise to find your gross profit. If you're running an enterprise such as a lawn-garden service, gross receipts and gross profit will be the same thing. Here are two examples:

1. Mail Order Business		2. Lawn-Garden Service	
Gross receipts for month	$1100.00	Gross receipts for month	$800.00
Cost of merchandise	700.00	Cost of merchandise	—
Gross profit	400.00	Gross profit	800.00

To make up a profit and loss statement for the month from here, simply list gross profit and expenses in separate columns and subtract to find net profit or loss. (See Figure 14-4)

If your profit and loss statement shows a loss, then examine each expense item and determine whether or not you can eliminate that item or reduce it. (See Figure 14-5)

During day to day and month to month business operations, it's impossible to tell whether or not you're spending too much or where. But laid out on paper you can see where the problems are and can work toward correcting them. In Figure 14-9, for instance, we have a spare-time business that "lost" $239.00 for that particular month. Going over the figures, we see that everything seems to be in line except the owner's draw and the supplies. Checking, we find the owner had purchased fifteen reams of typing paper at $8.00 a ream and several similar items. To make a "profit" he must cut this expense back and also reduce his draw. What a profit and loss statement does is let you examine each item individually.

Even when you're making a good profit, you can also examine each item to see if there's a possible saving. Any time you reduce expenses and maintain volume, you add to the profit.

Generally, a profit and loss statement applies only to buying and selling goods. Since, however, we want to use the simplest method possible and still have an effective analyzing tool, we have modified it to suit all part-time enterprises.

Other Business Records

As your operation gets bigger you can get more sophisticated by recording your sales or money taken in on a separate sheet and your purchases on another. (See Figures 14-6 and 14-7)

With these two records you can compare the performances of individual items or different parts or areas of your business. (See Figure 14-8) Other records can be kept, such as a petty cash journal, sales return and allowances journal and others, but the few records listed here are enough to enable you to do a good accounting job simply.

How To Set Up A Simple Money-Making Budget

In addition to knowing how well you're doing, a business must also know exactly how much it can spend on each expense item every month. Otherwise you have nothing to keep you from overspending.

To make sure all costs stay in line, you must make up a sample budget so you know exactly how much you can spend on each item and still wind up making money. Simply list all possible expenses, such as rent, advertising, wages, etc., and decide basically how much you can spend on each. That's one way.

The best way, however, is to decide first on the profit you want to make, estimate your volume and subtract your profit. This gives you the amount available for operating expenses. As long as you don't spend more than this amount you will make the desired profit. This amount must then be divided among each expense item.

Let's run through an example: (See Figure 14-9)

Say you're running a lawn/garden service and have twenty yards to maintain every month at $25.00 each. This gives you a $500 monthly income. You decide you want a 20 percent profit each month plus your draw. Subtract your $100 profit. This leaves $400 with which to pay expenses.

Here are the items you must pay:

>   storage rental
>   truck payment
>   labor (high school boys)
>   gasoline and oil (equipment and truck)
>   equipment payment
>   spray chemicals
>   office supplies
>   miscellaneous
>   advertising
>   owner's draw

The fixed expenses are: truck payments $45.00, equipment payments $25.00, gasoline and oil approximately $20.00, labor expenses $150, spray chemicals $10.00. This adds up to $250.00, leaving $150.00 for the remaining expenses. It can be divided up this way: office supplies $10.00, advertising $10.00, storage rental $20.00, owner's draw $100.00, miscellaneous $10.00. After you decide how much you can spend for each expense item, then draw up an operating budget for your month to month operation. Each time you add or subtract an expense item you will need to make up a new operating budget.

How To Use Records To Simplify Your Tax Problems

You can simplify your Federal tax problems considerably by keeping books which automatically give you the categories and amounts needed to fill in your Federal tax forms. Conversely, try to avoid headings or categories in your books that do not correspond to those found on the tax forms. Keeping surplus records simply complicates the problem and requires extra work. It's permissible, however, to keep itemized records of items that help pinpoint expenses. This includes such things as auto expenses, travel, office supplies, postage, etc.

I.R.S. form 1040 shows the following categories: *gross receipts inventory at beginning of year, merchandise purchases, labor costs, material and supplies, other costs including auto expenses, inventory at the end of year, depreciation, taxes on business and business property, rent on business property, repairs, insurance, legal and professional fees,* and *commissions.*

It's also possible to keep amortization, retirement plans, interest, bad debts, losses of business property, and depletion. With the possible exception of bad debts and interest, you won't run into these often in your spare-time business operations.

To make records simplify your tax problem then, go over each of these categories needed to fill out form 1040 and make sure your records either show these items directly or that you can figure them out simply and quickly by combining a few column totals or by making a few fast calculations. This one step alone will save you hours of work and many dollars at income tax time.

How To Make Records Propel
You To A Great Fortune

Your records can make big money for you, really big money, if you'll let them. All you need do is to follow their advice. Brig Stranton, for instance, a Los Angeles factory worker, began with $400 and ten hours of extra time each week to market a series of games he'd invented. The first, a card game, did well, and he was soon realizing $8000 a year gross. Turning this game over to a manufacturer's representative to market, he then launched four more games, getting them into production and personally contacting large chain buyers all across the nation. At the end of the second year, now working 35 hours a week in his spare time, Brig Stranton had boosted his income to almost $30,000 gross a year.

He then sat down with his books as explained in this chapter and costed each game out to see what kind of a profit each was making. The first, second, fourth and fifth were returning almost 40 percent profit after expenses. The third was barely making 5 percent. Studying the records more closely, Brig realized that material and labor costs on this game were so high that it would never return better than 8 percent. He then immediately dropped that game and replaced it with another, which started returning a solid 35 percent within eight months.

After that, he analyzed each added product separately and dropped those that failed to reach 30 to 35 percent. This way he eliminated the unprofitable operations and made all time and effort really pay off—all because he paid careful attention to his analysis records.

You must do the same thing. First, look over each expense item in your overall operation to see if there are any possible reductions. Then look at each phase or unit to make sure all are profitable. Keep those that show profit and eliminate the others immediately. By doing both operations relentlessly, searching your records to bring expenses down, and eliminating unprofitable operations, your records will literally propel you to riches. The more money you make, the better this system will work.

The key here is vigilance. It's not enough to discover at the end of the year that one phase or item isn't making money. You must know immediately. This requires constant checking. Check at the end of each month and weed out unprofitable areas.

A warning, however: Don't eliminate items that are just getting started and haven't yet had enough time to show a good profit. What you're looking for are those items that will never do well simply because of their cost structure or lack of a possible market. Time and experience alone will enable you to tell which these are.

An important adjunct to this system is the setting of desired profit. As explained earlier in this chapter, to make good money you must first decide what profit you must have, then figure expenses accordingly. In a part-time enterprise net profit must run somewhere between thirty and fifty percent. Anything less will make the accumulation of big money extremely slow and difficult.

The rule here, then, is to make exactly the profit you want, or don't bother to do it at all. By all means, let your records be your guide as to what you cut back or expand—they can truly propel you to a great fortune.

Sample Single Sheet Records
Sept. 1973

Date	Ck #	entry	money taken in	amount ck	draw	wages	professional services	inventory purchases	supplies	meals & travel	postage	insurance	advertising	rent utilities	misc.

Figure 14-1.

Spare-time businesses with employees should also add columns for withholding social security and any item required by the state.

Sample Single Sheet Records
Sept. 1973

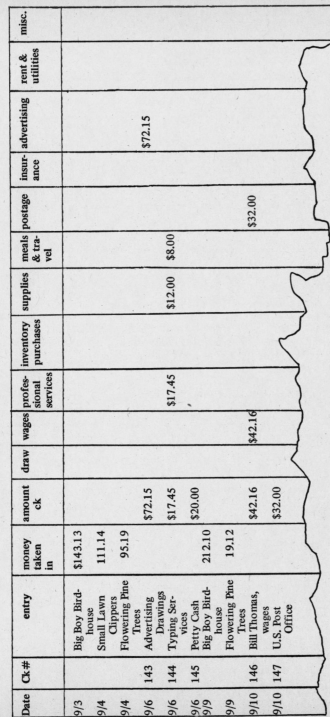

Date	Ck #	entry	money taken in	amount ck	draw	wages	professional services	inventory purchases	supplies	meals & travel	postage	insurance	advertising	rent & utilities	misc.
9/3		Big Boy Bird-house	$143.13												
9/4		Small Lawn Clippers	111.14												
9/4		Flowering Pine Trees	95.19												
9/6	143	Advertising Drawings		$72.15									$72.15		
9/6	144	Typing Ser-vices		$17.45			$17.45								
9/6	145	Petty Cash		$20.00					$12.00	$8.00					
9/9		Big Boy Bird-house	212.10												
9/9		Flowering Pine Trees	19.12												
9/10	146	Bill Thomas, wages		$42.16		$42.16									
9/10	147	U.S. Post Office		$32.00							$32.00				

Figure 14-2 Spare-time business with employees should also add columns for withholding social security and any item required by the state

PETTY CASH TICKET

9/6/71
Ck# 145

$20.00

(includes receipts for supplies
$4.00, $8.00 and $8.00 for a
business dinner.)

Figure 14-3

Figure 14-4

SAMPLE PROFIT & LOSS STATEMENT

Canoe Rental

Gross receipts from June rentals		$1500.00
Cost of merchandise		---
Gross profit		1500.00
	Expenses	
Owner's draw	$500.00	
Rent	50.00	
Utilities	35.00	
Advertising-brochures	80.00	
Insurance	14.00	
Payments on canoes	70.00	
Depreciation	10.00	
Supplies	15.00	
Misc. business exp	30.00	
Total expenses	804.00	(804.00)
Net profit or loss		696.00 profit

Figure 14-5

SAMPLE PROFIT & LOSS STATEMENT

Loss Analysis

Gross receipts from June rentals		$1500.00
Cost of merchandise		–––
Gross profit		1500.00
	Expenses	
Owner's draw	$1000.00	
Rent	100.00	
Utilities	35.00	
Advertising	80.00	
Insurance	14.00	
Payments on canoes	70.00	
Depreciation	10.00	
Supplies	400.00	
Misc. business expenses	30.00	
Total expenses	1739.00	(1739.00)
Net profit or loss		239.00 loss

Figure 14-6

Sales
Or Income From Services

Date	Item or Job #1		Item or Job #2		Item or Job #3	
	Quantity or time spent	Amount taken in	Quantity or time spent	Amount taken in	Quantity or time spent	Amount taken in

Figure 14-7

Purchases
or Costs
(Include both time put in and purchases
for a particular job)

Date	Supplier or individual	Item or Job	Quantity or hours	Unit cost	total cost	

Figure 14-8

ACCOUNTING FOR ITEMS OR AREAS

Items

Item	Sales		Cost	Gross Profit
Sales Price	$1.00			
Number sold	100			
Total volume sales	$100.00			
Total cost of item			$67.00	
sold-(from expense records				$23.00

Services

Item	Money Taken in		Cost	Gross Profit
Money Received	$500.00			
Total Cost			$202.00	
				$298.00

Figure 14-9

MONTHLY OPERATING BUDGET
Lawn Garden Service

Estimated monthly income	$500
Profit wanted 20% =	$100
Amount left for expenses	$400

sample budget

Item	estimated amount	amount actually spent
Storage rental	$20.00	
Truck payment	45.00	
High school boys labor	150.00	
gasoline and oil	20.00	
spray chemicals	10.00	
equipment payment	25.00	
office supplies	10.00	
advertising	10.00	
owner's draw	100.00	
misc.	10.00	
total	400.00	

Checking On Chapter 14

1. Good records are easy to keep with a minimum of effort.
2. Records increase your profits by telling you which activities to emphasize, which to eliminate. They tell you how much cash you have on hand, how much money you owe, what your expenses are, and how much profit you're making.
3. Books should be simple and include the money taken in, your draw, inventory purchases, supplies, meals and travel, expenses, gasoline, automobile expenses, insurance, postage, advertising, wages, professional services, miscellaneous expenses, and other needed categories. All money received or paid out should be recorded in your checking account.
4. Use a profit and loss statement to determine if you're making or losing money, and how much.
5. You can use other records to compare individual performances of different parts of your business.
6. Use a budget which decides first on the profit you want to make, then budget for expenses out of the money left.
7. Records should simplify your tax problems. Simply keep only those categories which are needed to fill our Federal income tax forms.
8. Records can propel you to even greater profits. Analyze each expense item to see if there are possible reductions. Then examine each phase or unit and eliminate unprofitable operations immediately.

Chapter 15

The Lifetime Plan for Continuous Fortune-Building

Up to this point we've talked about making big money through part-time enterprises. Now we want to find ways to take some of the profits made in your part-time business and make them work even harder. You can do this by investing. These investments can be conventional ones like real estate, stocks, bonds, mutual funds and others, or unconventional ones that you can get into easily with little money, yet still return a good profit.

In this chapter we'll look into some of the ins and outs of investing and learn how to make investments propel you to even greater riches.

How To Look For The Right Kind Of Investments

Not all investment opportunities will be right for you. Some will require more money than you want to invest, others will take too much time to manage, still others will be too risky. Here are some factors to consider:

(1) A good investment will be one that allows you to start with what you have available. This includes the amount of money you have to invest, the time you want to spend, the knowledge you have, the equipment you need and all else.

(2) A good investment will operate, at least part of the time, under its own momentum automatically. That is, you will not have to work at it as you do an ordinary business, putting in regular hours and specified periods of time.

(3) A good investment will contain a limited amount of risk. All investments contain some risk—some, however, are reasonable, while others are wild gambles.

George and Eric Templeton of Houston, Texas, are good examples of both of these. George and Eric were brothers with two thousand dollars each to invest. George weighed the risk of each investment, then put $1000 in mutual funds and $1000 in tube testers leased to retail stores.

Eric, on the other hand, backed two brothers who believed they could strike it rich mining gold in Idaho. The rest he invested in a 1000 mph. rapid transit system advanced as the lifetime dream of a local engineer.

George's mutual fund returned almost 7 percent a year, the tube tester investment 22 percent. Eric, however, never heard from the gold mining brothers again, and had to sue the engineer to get part of his money back.

(4) A good investment also feels right to you. This is hard to define, but after looking over all the available material and considering the possibilities, it simply seems to be the right course. In your investing career you will find some investments that fit the other three criteria listed here, but simply feel are wrong for you. While this may be unscientific, you'll be wise to avoid these and consider only those you can actually get excited about.

Where To Find Small Cash Investments

As soon as your part-time business starts producing extra, uncommitted cash, you should immediately start an investment program to get that money working again. The big problem for most small investors is where to find $50, $100, $200 and even $500 investments that produce good returns. Actually, they are all around you. We'll list several areas in this section that will help you get started. Here are some to consider:

Recreation or Spare-Time Rentals

What a wide open field this is—recreational rental investments include bicycles, snowmobiles, motorcycles, trailers, campers, canoes, ATV's and similar items. A recreational rental investment, however, is quite distinct from a recreational rental business. You simply buy the rental units, then place them in various locations for others to rent.

Douglas Toms, a Seattle, Washington businessman who quit his $7000 a year warehouse job and parlayed a borrowed $75 into an extremely lucrative $80,000 a year making Indian Tepees on special order, was looking for a safe way to pyramid his fortune without risk. One day Douglas happened to be reading a magazine article about the growing bicycle craze when he suddenly realized that there was extra money to be made from this sport. The next day he lined up a number of filling station operators who would let him place tandem bicycles on their lots for rent. The operator was to provide the lot, take care of the bicycles, keep records and rent them out. For this he gets a share of the profit. Douglas, however, must keep them in repair and check on each service station operator regularly to make sure he's handling his end of the operation. To date, Douglas has fifteen service stations renting bikes and takes in an extra $1500 a month over and above expenses.

This type of operation works well with any kind of small recreational vehicle or boat. You must buy the equipment in the first place, select the areas in which you want to rent, solicit service stations or other small businesses to handle the rentals, and service them regularly.

Service stations probably make the best rental locations for several reasons: there are a tremendous number to choose from, there's room on most service station lots to store and display the vehicles, and most service station operators are on the lookout for almost anything that will bring in added revenue.

Try to select rental locations with a good demand. Bicycles do well almost anywhere there is a place to ride, such as a park. Canoes and boats do well near lakes or rivers. Trailers, campers and tent trailers do well in almost any city location, since they will be pulled (or driven) to recreation areas. Snowmobiles and all-terrain vehicles rent best near where they'll be used.

You'll need a contract for anyone renting your equipment, including an agreement to provide the vehicles at a specified rate (usually the businessman handling the equipment will get from 40 to 50 percent of the total rental fee), the amount he can charge, the deposit he takes, if any, and the type or kind of protection he must provide the vehicles. Here also include provisions for records and upkeep of the vehicles.

You must also provide the businessman handling your vehicles with a standard record sheet that lists whom he has rented to, the number of hours rented and the fees collected.

You will need to establish regular times to collect your part of the fees and pick up vehicles needing repairs. You should also make spot checks to insure that the rentals are being reported accurately. You can buy new vehicles (including boats) through distributors at less than retail price. Find these by writing to manufacturers. These names are available at the library in the *THOMAS REGISTER,* and in such magazines as *Trailer Life,* 23945 Craftsman Rd., Calabasas, Calif. 91302; *Hardware Merchandiser,* 7300 N. Cicero-Lincolnwood, Chicago, Ill. 60646; *American Bicyclist and Motorcyclist,* 461 Eighth Ave., New York, N.Y. 10011. You can also find good used equipment buys by watching the classified section of your local newspaper.

Musical Instruments

Music interest today is on the increase, and children everywhere are taking lessons and participating in school bands as they never have before. Most parents, however, want the child to try out an instrument before they invest a large sum of money in it.

This is where your opportunity lies. The demand for musical instrument rentals to this group is booming, and they often keep the rental out for two months to two years.

Best investments are used instruments found through newspaper classified sections ($35 to $200 depending on the instrument). Use the same classified section to advertise your instruments for rent, from $5 to $10 per month.

Back Someone Else In A Spare-Time Business

People wanting to go into part-time business for themselves often need capital to start. These can be good investments provided you pick carefully. Advertise the fact that you have money available for a part-time business in the classified section of your local newspaper, then screen the prospects carefully, using the guides presented elsewhere in this book. Pick only those that look like they will make money. Draw up a written agreement (buy these at an office supply store) which includes your participation in the profits, usually 25 to 50 percent.

Using this method Steve Hester, a former $8000 a year janitor who opened a part-time dog grooming service with a $180 income tax refund and parlayed it quickly into a $15,000 a year enterprise, picked out five students at a local college, put up $1000 each, and went into partnership with each in a different kind of part-time business. These included a weekend car wash, a dance band, a day care center for student mothers, a mobile tire service and a college waterbed store. The combined income from these businesses now brings him $60,000 a year, four times his original income, without any extra work on his part.

Vacant Land Investments

Many cities today ban recreational vehicles (trailers, campers, motor homes) from parking either in driveways or on the streets in residential sections. Owners therefore must rent storage space elsewhere. People owning vacant lots in commercial areas also often welcome interim income while waiting to build or sell. These two factors can provide a good investment opportunity. You can rent or lease the land from the owner and rent out Rec V storage space.

Look up lot owners at the City Hall or the County Courthouse. Most investors try to keep monthly lot rental below $150 and charge Rec V owners from $8 to $15 a month storage (solicited through classified ads).

Many investors also hire a private police protection patrol ($20 to $50 a month) servicing other area merchants, so customers will feel their Rec V's are protected.

Resell Used Items

Not a typical investment but useful anyway if you're a shrewd buyer and seller. Look in the classified ads to see what a treasure trove is offered there: wheel chairs, space heaters, air compressors, snowmobiles, rototillers, cribs, reducing machines and a lot more.

One investor constantly scans these sections and buys items he feels are a good value. He then adds on a 30 percent profit for himself and re-advertises in the same classified section.

Although he must handle all sales himself, he often makes a 1000 percent profit on an initial $30 investment over a five or six month period. The trick is to buy the item below actual market value and resell at a profit. Not everyone has this knack, but those who do can make good investment profits.

Need-Filling Investments

This investment is similar to recreational rental investments, except it utilizes businesses other than service stations, and the item offered fills a need. Good examples of this are TV tube testers, copy machines, card plastic coating machines and similar items. These machines are placed in drug stores, grocery stores, hardware stores and similar retail outlets. You service machines at regular intervals and collect the money. As with recreational rentals, you need a written agreement between you and the store owner which spells out how much he receives, and what his obligations are as well as yours. You can often find these investments listed under *Business Opportunities* in the newspaper classified sections. Some investors are able to make returns up to 20 percent in this area. Often you can start with $500 to $1000 and add to it as you go along.

Equipment Rental Investments

Very similar to need-filling investments except the items placed in retail outlets are rented by the store's customers. This includes rug shampooers, floor buffers, exercise equipment, and similar items. Names of manufacturers selling these items can be found in *Rent-all Magazine,* 757 Third Ave., New York, N.Y. 10017.

It's possible to start here with as little as $150. Returns vary between 15 percent and 70 percent, depending on location, traffic and similar factors. Handle the contract between you and the retail store as you would for similar investments already listed here.

Bulk Lot Investments

This includes hay, firewood, peat moss, steer manure and many other items. This again is the buy and sell game. Bud Wilson, a $5,900 a year shoe salesman who needed extra cash to support his wife's parents, constantly watches for people felling and trimming trees. He then asks them if they want to sell him the wood. This he cuts into fireplace size and piles high on his front lawn. Backed up with a sign reading *firewood* it usually sells out in a short time. Normally, he figures on making $300 for every $100 he invests. Besides simply looking for homeowners cutting their own trees he also finds his firewood by advertising for it in the classified ads. This adds about $4300 a year to his income, which more than takes care of his wife's parents.

Another small investor, Jerry Keister, a Sacramento, California government clerk, does the same thing with bales of hay. He buys it from local farmers, adds 25¢ a bale, then stacks it on a vacant lot he's rented in a neighborhood with many horse owners. To make sales, he puts up a large sign which informs interested buyers that he's only there on Saturday and that they must haul the hay away themselves.

Frequently he sells four or five hundred bales a Saturday this way. His investment for this amount averages $400 to $500, his profit runs from $80 to $125. Not bad for part-time work on Saturdays!

Farm Machinery Investments

Farmers frequently need extra equipment such as tractors, disc harrows, and similar items. They also have a need for specialized crop handling equipment: rotary cutters, harvesters and more. The more specialized the equipment, the less likely the farmer is to buy it for himself and the more likely you will have a rental market for it.

This equipment can be expensive, however, running from $300 to as high as $17,000-$18,000 and more. Most items run considerably less. You can frequently invest several hundred down and put the rest on payments. Rental fees depend on your investment, but as a rule of thumb figure on making 30 percent a year on every dollar invested.

You can find used equipment by watching the ads under "farm equipment" in the newspaper. You can also find names and addresses of farm equipment manufacturers in *Southern Farm Equipment* magazine, PO Box 6429, Nashville, Tenn. 37122, or *Implement and Tractor* magazine, 1014 Wyandotte St., Kansas City, Mo. 64105.

Resort Area Re-Rentals

Currently cabin rentals in resort areas are booming for both summer and winter use. You can make money on the fact that the weekend or weekly rental rate is far greater than the all-season rate.

Greg Beachum, a San Francisco spare-time businessman and invester, originally was an $8600 a year bus driver but decided he wanted a lot more out of life than that. He sets aside $1000 every winter for ski rental investments. Last winter he rented two A-frame cabins for $500 each for the season, running from the last week in November to the second week in April. He then advertised them under *Mountain Houses—for rent* in the classified section of the paper for $125 a week, $75 a weekend. The results: one cabin brought $1500 for the season, the other approximately $1000, leaving a $1500 profit on his investment. The ads themselves ran continuously at a total cost of $51.

To find his investment cabins Greg advertises in the classifieds, asking to lease a cabin for the entire winter season. As the offers come in, he selects the area carefully and secures an agreement in writing that states he may rent the cabins or sub-lease them as he sees fit.

He also hires an older retired couple living near the cabins at $10 a job to clean up after each rental. His work consists of answering the phone and taking reservations. All rentals are payable in advance. Greg's total income for the year now approximates $59,000, out of which he maintains a large home, four cars and a large cabin of his own.

Don't Overlook Conventional Investments

Non-conventional investments frequently require less cash to start and sometimes bring higher returns, but you should also consider the possibility of conventional investments for the earnings from your spare-time businesses. These include second mortgages, land, mutual funds, limited partnerships, apartments and duplexes, houses, stocks, investment clubs, and loans. Let's look at each and see how they stand up as an investment.

Second Mortgages

Many people today need to borrow money to make the down payment on the home they want, or borrow money on their home for some purpose. You can loan them this $200, $300, $1000 or more, take a second mortgage on their home, get a return up to 18 percent a year and have a protected investment.

If your borrower defaults, you can foreclose the second. The bank or other institution holding the first mortgage must be paid first, but if you are cautious and don't loan more than an amount which together with the first mortgage will be under the market value of the house, your investment will be secure.

You can buy second mortgage agreements at an office supply store. You should also check a potential customer's credit. Often you can make an arrangement for this through the local Credit Bureau. Sometimes this is in the form of membership or a yearly contract. Your bank can also check credit for you. You can find potential prospects with a small ad under *Real Estate Loans* in your local paper.

Land

You can still make money buying small parcels of land and breaking them into two, three, or four parcels for resale. Start by looking for vacant land for sale in the newspaper classifieds. You must use your own judgment to determine if there's a market for small parcels where you want to buy. Local real estate firms can also advise you of the condition of this market, but don't rely solely on their advice.

Five acre parcels in this country can be bought for $100 to $15,000 or more depending on the location. A five acre parcel selling for $1000 can often be divided into four parcels and resold for $500 each.

Financing varies widely. You can sometimes put $50 down on a $1000 parcel and finance the rest at $25 to $50 a month. Typical, however, is $300 down and five to ten year financing at 8 percent to 10 percent interest.

Start by looking at as many parcels in your area as possible, and try to form some idea of the market for small lots. If you must hold for some time before reselling, consider (in figuring possible profits) the taxes, total interest, and payments.

Mutual Funds

The advantage of mutual funds is that they have professional money management, they reduce investment risk, and they spread their investment for safety. Funds can be classified by objectives such as growth or income, they can be classified by investments such as specialty funds (chemicals, electronics, aircraft, etc.), or balanced funds which invest in bonds as well as stocks. These funds ordinarily return from 2 percent to 7 percent and up annually.

Some funds have done moderately well during the current setback, others have fared badly. Best to check their brochures carefully and determine which have performed well. Either the book *Successful Investing Through Mutual Funds* by Robert Frank (Hart Publishing Co., 1969) or *What About Mutual Funds?* by John Straley (Harper and Row, 1967) can give you guidelines for doing this. You can obtain brochures by calling any broker listed in the telephone yellow pages or by answering ads in the Wall Street Journal. You can start your investment in some funds with a small amount of money. The books mentioned above will give you the details of how to start your investment and the factors to consider.

Limited Partnership Syndicates

Limited partnership syndication is simply the pooling of investment dollars by a large number of investors for the acquisition of land, apartments, buildings, or similar income-producing property. The structure consists of a general partner who manages the property and limited partners who share in the profits, but generally have no voice in management. You put specified amounts, usually from $500 up with monthly payments of between $25 and $50. You can find these limited partnerships advertised in the *Wall Street Journal* or on the financial pages of your local paper.

Apartments and Duplexes

More than one millionaire has made his entire fortune in apartment and duplex investments. A great advantage here is that you can start with a small investment ($500 to $3500) and expand as you save the cash. Real estate investment, however, is complicated, and a certain amount of expertise is needed. A good book, such as *How I Turned $100 Into A Million In Real Estate—In My Spare Time* by William Nickerson (Pocketbooks), *How To Build A Fortune In Real Estate* by Moser (Prentice-Hall), *How To Make Money In Real Estate* by McMichael (Prentice-Hall), or *How Real Estate Fortunes Are Made* by Bockl (Prentice-Hall) will help you through the pitfalls.

Stocks

Stocks can be a good investment area for your spare cash, but again there are many pitfalls. *Proceed cautiously.* A good way to start is to organize an investment club. This consists of your friends, neighbors, or anyone else who is interested in investing. You can put up as little as $50 in the beginning, plus a $15 to $100 a month investment.

After you have the club together, a stock firm (found in the telephone yellow pages) will usually assign a broker to your club. Don't expect to make big money from an investment club, but you can break in this way with little risk. From here you can advance to a larger investment portfolio of your own.

How To Make Investments Fit Your Money-Making Plans

After you start to accumulate some surplus cash, investments should always be a part of your money-making plans. The question is, however, how do you make them fit your other activities? The answer is to consider them on a time, labor, dollar, interest, and background basis. If they fit well in most of these areas, then you can probably handle them easily with a minimum of effort. Here are some pointers:

(1) *Consider your time involvement:* The more time you spend in work activities, the less you will want to spend managing an investment. For instance, if your part-time activities require thirty hours or more a week, you probably wouldn't want to spend more than one to ten hours extra in investment activity. On the other hand, if your part-time activities account for only ten hours or so a week, you might welcome a greater time involvement.

A mutual fund investment, for instance, would require almost no time. Recreation spare-time rentals, on the other hand, would require a great deal of personal supervision.

Here are the general time requirements for the investments discussed in this chapter:

> *Large time-consuming investments* — recreational rentals, reselling used items, need filling.
> *Medium time-consuming investments* — musical instruments, backing someone else, vacant land, equipment rental, bulk lot, farm machinery, resort area re-rentals, land, apartments and duplexes.
> *Little time-consuming investments* — mutual funds, second mortgages, stock. (Stock investments, however, can take large amounts of time, depending on your approach.)

In deciding whether or not an investment fits on a time basis, simply estimate how much time you feel you will need for a

particular investment activity, then add it to the time you're
already putting in. That will tell you whether or not you can handle
that particular investment easily.

(2) *Consider the labor needed:* Investments that require a lot of
activity go well with part-time enterprises that make few demands,
but are bad with spare-time projects that require a great deal of
work.

For instance, a 27-year-old Los Angeles factory worker named
Bruce Hamilton needed an extra income to bail out a down and
out brother. Bruce developed a very successful part-time gourmet
food mail order business that brought in almost $18,000 a year.
Bruce, however, did part of the processing himself, all of the
packaging and mailing, and most of the advertising. This required
considerable work.

When he got ready to expand into investments, he started a
television tube testing route with an extra $500 that required him
to make the rounds of 35 stores twice a week. Within eight weeks
Bruce was ready to collapse. He then sold the route at a profit and
put this money into mutual funds. Although his return isn't as
great, mutual funds fit better with his total activity.

Consider, then, how much actual work each requires and try to
match little spare-time work with an active investment, and active
spare-time projects with little time investments.

(3) *Consider the money needs:* Whether or not an investment
fits your money-making plans also depends on how much money
you have to invest, and how much a project takes. Unfortunately,
many investors forget this. Greg Randolph, a part-time ski clothing
manufacturer grossing almost $30,000 a year, had about $1000 to
invest. Unfortunately, he picked a snowmobile rental investment
that required $1800 initially, and another $1000 within two
months just to keep up with demand. This caused him to take
additional money from his part-time business and cut down on
supply orders. The result was that overall income dropped until he
caught up.

The rule, then, is to invest only extra or surplus money and not
draw any capital needed for the business itself. Otherwise the two
activities interfere and make each other more difficult.

(4) *Consider your own interest:* To be successful with your
investments, you must have an overall interest in that type of
investment. Henderson Biggot, for instance, a successful part-time

printer who ran a $300 investment and fifteen hours a week into a $50,000 a year enterprise, couldn't seem to get interested in stocks, yet was convinced by his friends that here is where he should put his money.

As a result, Henderson didn't take enough interest to learn anything about stocks, didn't follow them regularly, or go over his portifolio periodically to weed out the losses.

When his loss at the end of the first year hit $5000, Henderson recognized his mistake, took his money out of the stock market and invested it in duplex rental units. This kind of an investment intrigued him so much he enrolled in a real estate class at a local college, started reading at length about rental investments, and began to look for more duplexes to acquire. At the end of the second year Henderson had recouped his loss and made an additional $2000 profit.

Unfortunately, interest has a great deal to do with just how successful you will be with particular investments. And in order to make investments fit your money-making plans, you must ignore those that hold no interest and consider only those you're willing to work with and learn something about.

(5) *Consider your background:* Your background is important in making your investments fit your money-making plans. A background that has something to do with your investment area can often increase your overall investment income considerably.

Dennis Ralston is a San Francisco high school teacher who had played in his grade school, high school and college bands. In addition to teaching, Dennis spent twenty hours a week operating a $25,000 a year part-time advertising service. He had started this business with $100 to pay off some bad debts when his father's business failed. Dennis also found time to compose music and spent considerable time reading about musicians. When he decided to invest $300 in the rental of used musical instruments, he discovered much to his surprise that his background really came in handy.

First, Dennis could talk music and was able to advise parents whether or not he thought their child could be a successful musician and with what instrument. In addition, he was so enthusiastic about music that he often convinced the parents that one of them should take up an instrument at the same time their children did. Also, parents were so impressed with his background and knowledge they sent many friends to him. Within a short time his instruments were booked months in advance, and at the end of the first year his $300 investment had returned well over $3000—enabling him to put a down payment on an airplane he'd been dreaming about for years.

Ron Rouse, on the other hand, a discount store clerk who skyrocketed a $400 investment in a part-time ski cap manufacturing business to an over $150,000 a year gross income, did equally well in the stock market. Ron's father had been interested in stocks all his life and frequently talked over investments with his son. In addition, Ron had spent two years working for the local newspaper as part-time business and financial reporter. During this time he received a thorough grounding in stocks. He read the financial news daily and had a good working knowledge of the language.

When he finally accumulated investment cash, he naturally thought of the stock market. He immediately found he had a natural feel for this type of investment and within a short time bought $600 worth of stock in an automotive hard parts company. Six months later he sold that stock for $1000 profit and invested the entire amount in two recreational vehicle firms. By the end of the year he had purchased twelve stocks and sold six. Although some did better than others, his overall profit amounted to almost $3000. Ron's background probably didn't account for his entire success, but it certainly helped.

How To Test Your Investment Possibilities

There are many kinds of investments. Some will make money, others won't. Investments, however, shouldn't be a guess. Before spending your money you should have some idea of how your investment will do and just what kind of return you can expect.

There are, of course, no accurate formulas, but here are a few guidelines you can follow:

Figure out the possible dollar potential on paper. This is the first step. Naturally it is a guess, but you must start somewhere. Let's take used musical instruments as an example. We find, for instance, that we can buy three cornets and three clarinets (used) for $300. They then rent for $15 a month, $1080 gross a year. Divide your initial investment plus any major expenses for that year into the year's gross. For the musical instruments, this is 360 percent. To find the practical possibilities of this investment, now divide it by three, for 120 percent.

Say also that you are considering the possibility of a mutual fund that invests in Government bonds for a 7 percent a year return. Just how do these two stack up? It's impossible to tell at this point. Don't try to make any comparisons. Simply find your possible percentage of gross profit. Next, rate the possible return on this return index. (See Table 1)

Table 1

3 to 5%	1
6 to 10%	2
11 to 30%	4
31 to 50%	8
51 to 100%	12
101 to 200%	20
200% and above	30

We will use these figures later to give us an investment index. On this table, the musical instruments rate 20, the mutual fund 2. Go through this procedure for any investments you're considering except stocks. These require a much more complicated analysis. Pick up a book on stocks at any bookstore to help you make your decisions here.

To find the practical net return possibilities, divide musical instrument possible gross for the year by 3 (as we did here), recreational rentals 2, backing someone else 4, vacant land improvements 3, reselling used items 3, need filling investments 3, equipment rental 3, bulk lot investments 2, farm machinery investments 4, resort area re-rentals 4, second mortgages 2, land 2, mutual funds 1, apartments and duplexes 2.

When considering apartments and duplexes, you should be a little more precise than is possible with the above method. Here is a formula that will give you a more accurate dollar potential:

First, estimate your possible yearly rents in dollars. Jot this figure down on a piece of paper, and from it subtract the total cost of your taxes and utilities. This will give you your expected annual income.

If the rent is to be over $200 a month, put down twice the monthly rental. If the building's interior or exterior is in bad shape, deduct 10 percent of the expected annual income. If the yard or grounds around the building are rundown, deduct another 1 percent.

Estimate the value of the location—the building's closeness to schools, stores, etc. If it is in a good location, make no deduction, but if the location is only fair, deduct 5 percent, and if it is poor, deduct 10 percent of the expected annual income. The same is true of the character of the neighborhood—if you rate it "good," make no deduction, but if it is only fair, deduct 5 percent, and if it is poor, deduct 10 percent of the expected annual income.

Add up all the deductions and subtract the figures from the total of the expected annual income, then multiply the remaining figure by seven. This gives you the estimated fair market value.

To get a table value, first find the percentage of income return for your duplex or apartment by dividing your total dollar investment into the total possible return minus the deductions. For example, You put $1000 down on a $20,000 duplex in a fair location in a fair neighborhood. The rent is $150 each side.

The possible yearly income minus taxes here,	$3000
Deductions for location and neighborhood	$300
	$2700

To get a percentage of gross profit return, Divide $1000 into $2700. This gives us 270 percent. Now by following our practice of dividing apartments and duplexes by two to find the practical net percentage return, we get 135 percent. This gives us a figure on the return index (Table 1) of 20.

However, this needs adjusting. When we multiply the $2700 income by 7 to get a fair market value we get $18,900. That's the price we should have paid. But since we overpaid we must subtract from the return index. (See Table 2)

Table 2. Amount paid over or under market value

$5000 over fair market value	-15
$2000 to $4999 over	-10
$1000 to $1999 over	- 8
$ 500 to $ 999 over	- 6
$ 100 to $ 499 over	- 4
$ 100 to $ 499 under market value	+ 4
$ 500 to $ 999 under	+ 6
$1000 to $1999 under	+ 8
$2000 or more under	+10

Since we paid $1,100 too much we should subtract 8 points from our 20 to give us *12* on the possible return index table.

We must also treat land separately. Make up a numbered checklist on a sheet of notepaper and rate each factor as "excellent," "good," or "fair."

Table 3. Checklist For Successful Land Investment

Population
   1. present population area
   2. 10 year population projected growth
Accessibility
   3. Existing freeways
   4. Planned freeways
   5. Airports
   6. Railroads
Employment
   7. Industry
   8. Construction
   9. Tourist
   10. Commercial Business
Water
   11. Existing
   12. Planned
Climate
   13. average summer
   14. summer high
   15. winter low
   16. amount of rainfall
Topography
   17. Level, compared to sea-level
   18. Grade of hills
Recreation
   19. hunting
   20. fishing
   21. boating
   22. skiing
   23. ocean
   24. golf
Metropolitan area
   25. distance
        (Within 0-50 miles is excellent, 50-100 miles is good, 100-150 miles is fair)

26. population size

(Over 100,000 is excellent, 25,000 to 100,000 is good, under 25,000 is fair)

To use this chart effectively, find the possible percentage return on your land investment per year. Check with local real estate offices to find about how much raw land has been increasing per year in your area, then figure the percentage increase on your investment. For instance, if land in your part of the city has been increasing 10 percent in value every year and you can buy an acre for $1000 with $200 down, you can reasonably expect your lot to be worth $1100 in a year—which means you received $100 for your $200 investment, or a 50 percent increase. To find practical return possibilities, divide by 1 to give you 50 percent.

Now, however, you must deduct from the checklist for successful land investment. Grade each category: population, accessibility, etc. Subtract one percentage point for each two "good" ratings, and one point for each "fair" rating. Next look up the return index in Table 1.

Make a sample investment. Sometimes you will actually make a trial investment, other times you can dry run. You can, for instance, buy one musical instrument and try renting it. The investment is small, but you don't want to invest $1800 in a trailer just to see how it will go. You can, however, do it by "proxy." Many small rental yards keep one or two trailers for rental. Spot one, and over a three month period keep track of how many times that particular trailer is out. This will take work, but it may well mean money in your pocket in the long run.

In the meantime, call the rental yard for their rates. Look up the address of that particular trailer manufacturer in the Thomas Register (found in the Library Reference Room). Write him for the wholesale price for rental purposes or ask to be referred to a distributor who can give you a price. Once you have a cost figure and know how much a particular yard made in a three month period, you can figure out possible yearly income and a possible percentage of return. Compensate for the time of year you took your sample. Summer rentals are best, spring and fall only fair, winter poor. Now let's take an example:

Say you discover you can buy a trailer at $1200 with $200 down and $50 a month (through a bank loan). You also discover that one firm renting these trailers has them out about twenty weeks a year at $50 a week ($1000). Subtract your total payment of $600 for the first year from your probable return and you have $400 left. On an initial investment of $200 this gives you a 100 percent return. Going by our rule again, however, divide it by two for 50 percent and look up the return index in Table 1. It comes out to 8.

To figure the returns on other types of investments you will need some imagination, but basically you must spot someone doing something similar and observe him as closely as possible over a several month period.

Get outside opinions. If possible go to an outsider who knows something about what you want to do and who will give you an opinion. If you're considering an investment in television tube testers, for instance, go to a small business owner who has one in the store and ask him for an opinion. For resort re-rental call cabin owners listed in the paper and ask what they think. For second mortgage investments try to find someone with experience and ask his opinion. These people should not particularly be experts, but simply someone with some knowledge about these particular investment areas. Now rate them as to what they think: good, fair, poor. Assign ten points for good, five for fair, nothing for poor.

Go to the experts. Try to find someone who really knows something about your investment area. With recreational rentals, for instance, go directly to a rental operator and ask his opinion. Consider these opinions only as a part of your evaluation, however. Since many times "experts" have their own interests at heart or fail to see the overall picture of what you're trying to do, their opinions have only limited value. To get opinions on real estate or second mortgages, go to your local banker. For stocks and mutual funds, go to a local brokerage firm. Here are some other possibilities: musical instruments, a local music store renting instruments; backing someone else, your local banker; vacant land, a real estate broker; used items, a second-hand store; need filling, go to firms who are in the business; rental equipment, rental equipment firms; bulk lot investments, talk to people advertising this item in the newspaper classified; farm machinery, go to a rental firm specializing in farm equipment.

As before, rate these opinions good, fair, and poor—assign ten points for good, five for fair, and nothing for poor.

Look within yourself. Finally, ask yourself how you really feel about this investment and give it as honest a rating as you can, again grading good, fair, and poor—assigning ten points for good, five for fair, and nothing for poor. Don't try to do this, however, until you have completed all other ratings. After you have worked with this investment awhile you will begin to understand just how good it is. Unless you have spent time doing the other ratings honestly and in complete detail, however, you simply will not have accumulated the experience necessary for an accurate opinion.

Now we are ready to make an evaluation. Add all the points together. This includes the return index number from figuring out the dollar percentage potential and the sample investment, plus the ratings of knowledgeable people, experts, and yourself. Now divide by the total number of items used for your evaluation. You may leave out one evaluation item if you like.

Before making your final evaluation, consider one other factor—the stability of the investment. A savings account, for instance, is extremely stable, gambling unstable. When you have completed your initial calculations (obtained by adding all the points together from the dollar percentage potential, the sample investment, knowledgeable people, experts, and your own opinion), then add a stability factor to this, obtained from the Stability Table (Table 4).

Table 4. Stability Table

Recreational rentals	3
Musical instruments	2
Backing someone else	0
Vacant land improvements	4
Reselling used items	3
Need filling investments	3
Equipment rental	3
Bulk lot investments	2
Farm machinery investments	2
Resort area re-rentals	0
Second mortgages	5
Land	8
Mutual funds	10
Apartments and duplexes	10

Now evaluate your investment chances—The sum of the investment possibilities and the stability factor from Table 3, on the Investment Success Table (Table 5).

Table 5. Investment Success Table

0 to 5	bad
6 to 9	poor
10 to 15	fair
16 to 20	good
21 to 30	very good
30 and above	excellent

Let's look at a few examples:

We decide to go into resort re-rentals in California and find we can rent a cabin on a yearly basis for $200 a month. We estimate we can re-rent it reasonably, 35 weeks out of the year at $180 a week. This figure is obtained by surveying nearby cabin owners. Our total investment, then, is $2400, our total possible income $6300, or 262 percent on our investment. To find the possible net return possibilities, we divide by four (as noted earlier in this chapter). This gives us 65 percent. We then look up the investment index in Table 1, giving an investment index of 12. Since taking a sample is extremely hard in this case, we eliminate that step. Other cabin owners tell us that this investment is just fair because of having to clean up after each rental (5 points), local real estate people say the investment is only fair (5 points), and we ourselves evaluate it as fair (5 points). Now add it all together:

Dollar potential investment index	12
Knowledgeable people's opinion	5
Expert's opinion	5
Your opinion	5
total	27
Divide by 4 = approx	7
Add the stability factor from Table 3	0
total	7

Now look up the success possibility or investment rating in Table 5. This investment then rates poor.

Let's compare this to a mutual fund yielding 7 percent per year. This gives us a return index of 2 from Table 1, other investors rate this as good (10 points), experts rate it as good (10 points) and we rate it as good (10 points).

Dollar potential investment index	12
Knowledgeable people's opinion	5
Expert's opinion	5
Your opinion	5
total	27

Divide by 4 = approx.	7
Add the stability factor from Table 3	0
total	7

Dollar potential investment index	2
Knowledgeable people's opinion	10
Expert's opinion	10
Your opinion	10
total	22

Divide by 4 =	8
Add the stability factor from Table 3 =	10
total	18

Table 5 then indicates the investment is good.

How To Get The Most Out Of Every Investment

Making your investment pay off means managing your investments efficiently. This involves keeping your dollars working at all times, keeping good investment records, shifting your money from unprofitable investment areas, reviewing investments regularly, soliciting referrals, being alert to the possibilities of selling at a profit, and having an investment plan. Let's look at each separately.

Keep Your Dollars Working

Unless you keep constant watch, it's possible for some of your investment dollars to stop working. Brieghton Reynolds, for instance, a Denver government worker who parlayed a $300 nest egg into a $35,000 a year book mail-order business, decided to invest in bicycle rentals at a number of local service stations. Brieghton, however, had his money invested a full six months before he discovered that one station locked the bikes up during the week and refused to rent any day but Saturday. This in effect tied up his working dollars for six days a week. He then moved the bikes to another service station and immediately upped his overall return by 5 percent.

This rule applies to every kind of investment. If, for instance, a homeowner stops paying on a second mortgage, he in effect has tied up your working dollar. If you do not bring this mortgage current immediately, you have lost the use of that money for re-investment purposes, plus any collection costs you may have.

To keep your money working, then, you must review constantly and stay on the alert for problem areas.

Keep Good Investment Records

Records in investing are as important as any other business record. You must always know where your money is and just how much it's making.

When Brieghton Reynolds started his bicycle investment, he put ten bikes out to each station. Shortly afterwards, however, several stations asked for more, a few wanted some bikes removed, and others wanted some bikes taken back and others brought out. Since Brieghton did not keep exact inventory records of where his bikes were and did not record each transaction, he soon lost track of just who had how many bikes. As a result, when his overall count showed five bikes missing he had no way of knowing which station was responsible. He simply had to assume the loss himself and vow to keep better records in the future.

You should, then, keep records showing how much you've invested, exactly what you've invested in, how many units you have, what the costs are, and where each piece of equipment or investment unit is, plus anything else needed to help keep track of your money.

Shift Money From Unprofitable Investment Areas

At the end of the first year in the bicycle rental business, Brieghton Reynolds decided to add a few All Terrain Vehicles at some outlying areas. Within four months, however, Brieghton found the ATV's weren't renting and that each was losing money.

Instead of trying to keep these vehicles going, he immediately advertised and sold them at a $300 loss, putting the remaining money back into bicycles. While Brieghton did take a loss, at least he got his money working profitably again. This is what you must do. Review each area every month and get rid of those areas that aren't making money and look as if they won't for a long period of time.

Review Investments Regularly.

Unfortunately it's impossible at any time to invest money and forget it. You must constantly keep on top of what's going on. At the end of the first year with Brieghton Reynold's bicycle investment, for instance, bicycle rentals dropped off in several areas. Brieghton, however, was concerned with other things. He had turned the servicing and collection over to someone else several months before and didn't realize what was happening. As a result he did nothing. When Brieghton finally woke up to what was going on, bicycle rentals at three stations were losing money and just breaking even at one other. This principle of reviewing investments regularly applies to all investment areas. Conditions can change, and you'd better be aware before it costs you money.

Solicit Referrals

Not all investments lend themselves to referrals, but many do. People you hold second mortgages for can send friends for this kind of financing, bicycle rental customers can refer others, people who use photocopy services can talk about it, and so forth. The rule is, simply ask people you come in contact with to refer others. For less personal investment areas you can use brochures or printed solicitation.

Sell When You Can Make A Good Profit

After two years of bicycle rentals, Brieghton received an offer from a firm to buy his complete bicycle investment for $25,000. This was several times the $3000 he had put in. Therefore he sold, took the money, put $3000 into a similar investment enterprise in a neighboring city and invested the rest in stocks and mutual funds. Selling is, in effect, pyramiding. You can then take this money, start again somewhere else, and still have money left for additional investing. The rule is, however, don't sell until you can at least double the total amount you've put in.

Have An Investment Plan

Always have a general idea of where you want to go. If you've decided to invest in bicycle rentals, for instance, you might lay out a plan that says you'll establish fifteen rental stations in your city, then spread to three neighboring communities. After this you'll add motorcycles, snowmobiles, and small trailers to your rental line.

This kind of planning lets you know about where you're going next, avoids duplication, and in some cases allows you to save money by making similar expenditures only once instead of three or four times. All plans, however, should be flexible, since you want to be able to keep your money growing and withdraw from any area that looks like a loser.

How To Pyramid Every Investment

Investments themselves will, of course, make money. But you can make even more by using pyramiding techniques that will double and triple effective multiplying power of your investments. Here are some techniques you can use:

Put Profits Back In

Investment profits working for you can produce that much more income. Ray Mendals, a San Francisco utility worker, parlayed a $200 investment into a $100,000 a year part-time candle business. He then invested $1000 in an older duplex, and saved all profits until he had an additional $1000, and bought another duplex. Within 3 years Ray had 15 duplexes, and a gross investment income of $4000 a month. Investment profits re-invested simply help you reach your money goals that much faster.

Sell And Buy Regularly

Once you start investing, you'll find that there is a regular buy and sell cycle that will enable you to make additional money. Good activity always makes your investment go up. Ray Mendals learned this early in the game. He bought an older duplex for $15,000, invested another $200 in paint, then rented it for $130 each side. He then put an ad in the local paper advertising it for sale at $18,000. Within three hours after the paper came out, he sold it at full price. With the profit, he simply turned around and bought 3 more duplexes. Practically every investment has a time when it's worth more than you initially invested. Try to become aware of this increase and offer your investment for sale at that time, provided you can at least double the amount of money you put in.

Use Leverage Whenever Possible

Leverage simply means controlling as much money as possible with a minimum of your own cash. Say you buy $10,000 worth of land for 10 percent down ($1000) and it increases 50 percent in value within three years. You then sell this land, take your $5000 plus equity, and invest in land worth $50,000. You in effect control $50,000 with only $1000 of your own money (plus payments). Try to do this with every investment you make. Keep your original investment and payments as low as possible while acquiring as much cash value as possible.

Use The Pyramid Method

Good pyramiding requires both leverage and an increase in value of your investment. This method is often used to good advantage with land, but it can be applied to other investments also.

Let's say you buy an acre parcel for $2000 with 10 percent down and it increases 50 percent in three years. You then take your $1000 plus equity and buy a twelve acre parcel for $10,000 (with $1000 down). This is leverage. You then subdivide your parcel into twelve one-acre lots and sell them for $2000 each, or $24,000, leaving you with approximately $14,000. You then take half of this, buy fifty acres and start subdividing all over again. Using this method, some sharp land investors over the last ten years have managed to run an original $1000 into well over a million.

The secret here is to divide your investment into smaller pieces, selling at a larger amount per unit than you could get for these same units when sold as a larger piece. Pyramiding works well in many investment areas and can increase profits spectacularly.

Try To Make One Investment Lead To Others

One investment should actually trigger another. Once you start investing in duplexes, for instance, you almost automatically start looking for the next, and if you let it be known you're in the market they'll come to you.

This is true in most other areas. Bicycle rentals, for instance, lead almost automatically to motorcycles, ATV's and other recreational rentals. And once you let the word out that you're open to other locations and items, they'll automatically start coming to you. Simply talk about it to anyone who seems interested.

Keep These Investment Factors In Mind

Investments, like all other aspects of business, follow certain rules. Here are several you should keep in mind as you start your investment activity:

Don't invest until you have extra money: Investment money should be extra money. Money taken from your business that will hamper or slow it down creates a further problem.

Consider your investment expenses: Investment expenses must be kept low if you expect to make money. Avoid any investments which require monthly expenditures in excess of 3 percent of your original investment (payments on the investment itself excepted).

Make sure that borrowed money makes money: Borrowed money has one purpose, to make more money. Do not borrow money for living expenses, office extras or frills. Borrow only when you intend to re-invest for greater profits.

Watch the economy closely: Some investments bring better returns at some times than at others. When the economy slows down, for instance, some recreational activities also slow down. In addition, second mortgages return more on the investment when money is harder to get. The need for apartments and duplexes also goes up and down depending on local conditions. Watch closely how your particular investment behaves and react accordingly.

Make sure your investment produces a better percentage return than that same money would make invested in your spare-time business. If your investment money produces just as well in your business, then you might as well keep it there in the first place. Investments must produce a greater return to be worthwhile. Check this closely before investing.

Checking On Chapter 15

1. You can make even more money by re-investing.
2. A good investment does the following:

　　a. It allows you to start with the money and time you have

available.
b. It operates partially under its own momentum.
c. It contains limited risk.
d. It simply feels right

3. The following investments can be started with a small amount of money:

    a. Recreational or spare-time rentals
    b. Musical instruments
    c. Backing someone else
    d. Vacant lands
    e. Reselling used items
    f. Need filling investments
    g. Equipment rentals
    h. Bulk lot items
    i. Farm machinery
    j. Resort area re-rentals

4. The following conventional investments should also be considered:

    a. Second mortgages
    b. Land
    c. Mutual funds
    d. Apartments and duplexes
    e. Stocks

5. Investments should fit your needs in the following areas:

    a. The time required
    b. The labor needed
    c. The money needed
    d. Your interests
    e. Your background

6. Investments should be tested in the following ways:

    a. Figure out the possible dollar potential
    b. Make a sample investment
    c. Get outside opinions
    d. Get expert opinions
    e. Look within yourself

Rate each, add the stability factor, and evaluate the investment chances on the Investment Success Table.

7. To get the most out of every investment you should:

   a. Keep your dollars working
   b. Keep good investment records
   c. Shift money from unprofitable investment areas
   d. Review investments regularly
   e. Solicit referrals
   f. Sell when you can make a good profit
   g. Have an investment plan

8. Investments should be pyramided the following ways:

   a. By putting the profits back in ·
   b. By selling and buying regularly
   c. By using leverage whenever possible
   d. By using the pyramiding method
   e. By making one investment lead to another

9. When investing keep these investment factors in mind:

   a. Don't invest until you have extra money
   b. Consider your investment expenses
   c. Make sure borrowed money makes money
   d. Watch the economy
   e. Make sure your investment produces a better percentage return than that same money invested in your spare-time business.

Selected Book List

A Guide To Successful Investing, D'Ambrosio, Prentice-Hall
The Profit Magic of Stock Transaction, Hurst, Prentice-Hall

How To Buy Recreational Land For Profit, Bittney, Prentice-Hall
A Professional Guide To Commodity Speculation, Shaw, Parker
Publishing Co.

How To Buy Stocks, Engle, Little Brown
What About Mutual Funds, Straley, Harper

Index

Index

A

Abilities:
adding machine, 45
advertising, 42
application, 41
assembling small things, 42
bookkeeping, 42
business initiative, 42
carpentry, 42
cash register, 45
clerical, 42
construction, 42
contracting, 42
crafts, 42
decorating, 40
designing houses, 42
diagnosis, 42
energy, 40
fact fitting, 36-37
general design, 43
general management, 43
general selling, 43
goals, 40-41
hand and finger speed, 37-38
ideas, 35-36
inspection of production, 43
insurance, 43
keeping production going, 43
lab work, 43
making surveys, 43
managing production, 43
music memory, 39, 44
newspaper work, 44
number memory, 39-40
nursing, 44
observation, 38-39
pattern memory, 39

Abilities *(cont.)*
people-centered personality, 35
plumbing, 42
record keeping, 36
research, 44
secretarial work, 45
self-centered personality, 35
small tool handling, 38
stockroom work, 44
supervision, 44
taking complaints, 44
teaching, 44
three dimension factor, 37
type setting, 45
typing, 45
working with musicians, 45
writing from accumulated
facts, 45
Accounting, cost, 42
Accounts, delinquent, 28
Action, 18
Action plan, 90-91
Actionizing plan, 155-156
Activities:
infrequent, 125
necessary, 125
outside, 135-136
regular, 125
"Ad" test, 84-85
Adding machine, 45
Advertising, 18, 21, 23, 24, 29-30,
42, 64, 69-70, 91, 99-100,
122, 141
Afraid, being, 56-57
Agencies, government, 23
*American Bicyclist and
Motorcyclist*, 178
Amount, desired, 17, 18
Answering services, 62-73

205